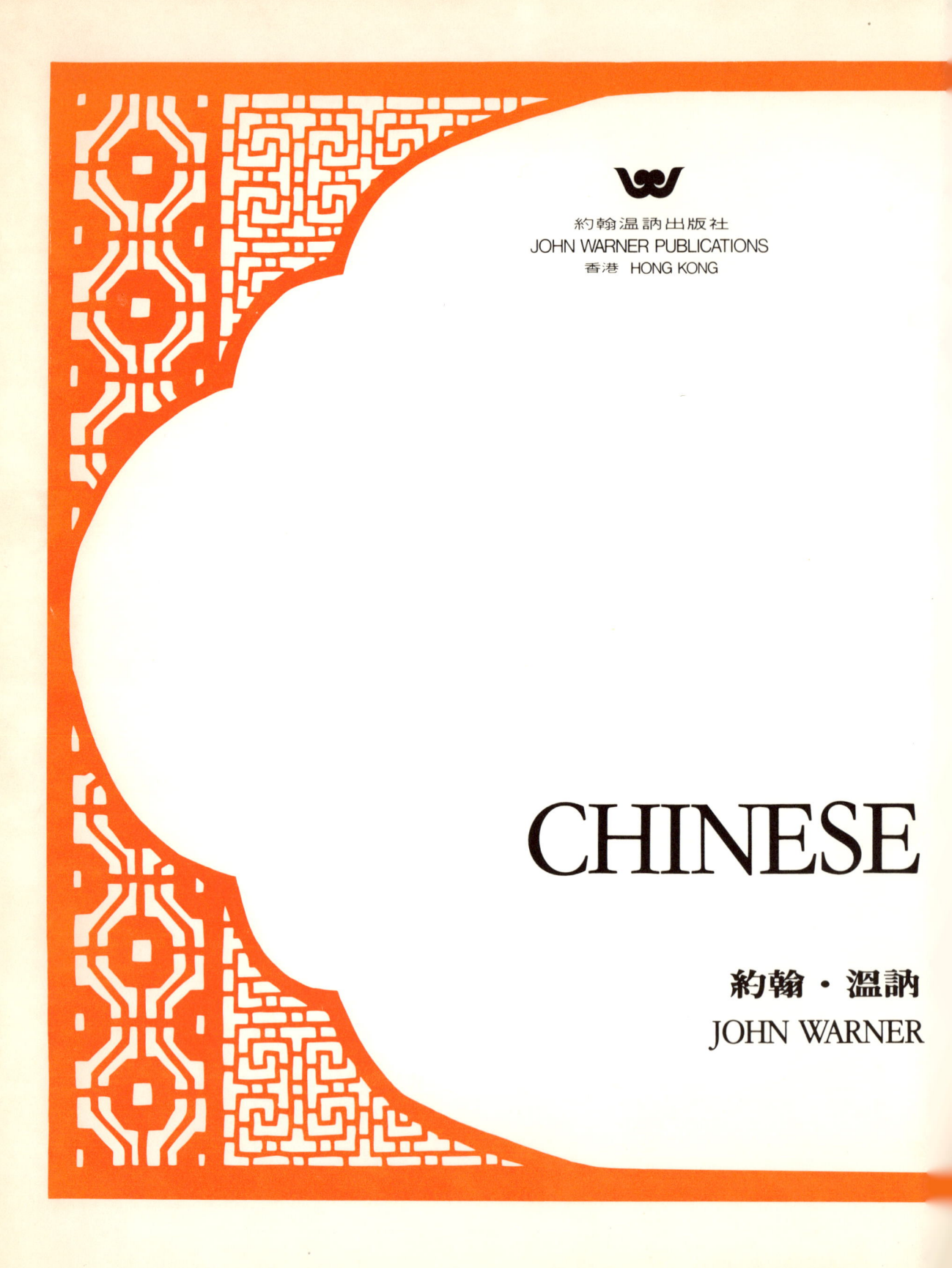

約翰溫訥出版社
JOHN WARNER PUBLICATIONS
香港 HONG KONG

CHINESE

約翰・溫訥
JOHN WARNER

中国剪纸
PAPERCUTS

First Edition 1978
Published by John Warner Publications
P.O. Box 6751, General Post Office, Hong Kong

Copyright © 1978 by John Warner Publications
All Rights Reserved
ISBN 962-7015-03-2

Printed in Hong Kong by Everbest Printing Co.

一九七八年初版

出版者：約翰・溫訥出版社
　　　　香港郵政總局
　　　　郵政信箱六七五一號

版權所有　不准翻印

香港恆美印刷有限公司承印

Contents 目錄

8	Origin and Use	
13	Chinese Symbolism	
17	Technique	
22	Map of China	

22	中國地圖
24	創造與利用
26	中國象徵主義
28	剪紙的技巧

34	Hopei	河北
36	Peking	北京
42	Weihsien	蔚縣
44	Tientsin	天津

| 50 | Shantung | 山東 |

	58	Shansi	山西
	66	Shensi	陝西
	68	Northern Shensi	陝北
	76	Southern Shensi	陝南
	82	Hupei	湖北
	96	Kiangsu	江蘇
	98	Nanking	南京
	110	Yangchou	揚州

	116	Chekiang	浙江
	118	Loching	樂清
	128	Yuhuan	玉環
	136	Other Places	其他地方

	148	Fukien	福建
	150	Amoy	廈門
	154	Chuanchou	泉州

	158	Kwangtung	廣東
	160	Foshan	佛山
	176	Chaochou	潮州

	186	Acknowledgement	鳴謝
	187	Index	索引

Origin and Use

Around the first century A.D., the Chinese invented that most flexible, versatile and adaptable of materials — paper. For several hundreds of years it probably remained precious and rather scarce, its use for daily and decorative purposes being severely restricted.

In 1959, at an archaeological site in an old city south of the Tarim Basin in the Yutien County of Sinkiang, the earliest known papercut in the form of a rosette was discovered (Fig. 1). The site dates back to the period known as the Northern and Southern Dynasties (A.D. 386-581) and the papercut may have been used as a design for the decoration of lacquer ware and architectural detail of this period. At the same site fragments of indigo blue and white cloth were also found.

It seems likely that earlier papercuts were not designs and pictures but auspicious Chinese characters. In the *Miscellany of Yu Yang*, 酉陽雜俎 it is stated that it was the custom for women in the Northern Dynasties to hang papercut characters 宜春 (*i-chun*) meaning 'fine for spring', on their doors on the first day of spring.

In the T'ang Dynasty (A.D. 618-906) papercuts are the subject of a poem by the poet Ts'ui Tao-yung and from other sources of this period they are described as being used to decorate plants and worn by ladies in their hair in the form of butterflies and flowers. Papercuts were also used as decorations for food, particularly cakes which hikers would carry with them to high vantage points during the Chung Yang Festival. This custom is mentioned in the *Record of the Dreamy Splendours of the Eastern Capital* 東京夢華錄 (*Tung Ching Meng Hua Lu*) written in the Southern Sung Dynasty (1127-1279). There is also an account which appears in the *Miscellany of the Chih-ya Hall*, 志雅堂雜鈔 written by Chou Mi in the thirteenth century, of an eccentric young man who cut characters and flower patterns into the long and voluminous sleeves of his gown.

Certainly by this time the use of papercuts was widespread and the subject matter to be found included representations of the animals, birds and flowers of the country-side as well as mythological, historical and theatrical characters and symbols from Buddhist and Taoist religions.

Twenty or so years ago the majority of windows in China were still made of paper as they had been a thousand years earlier. Pasted damp over a wooden lattice frame, the paper became taut when dry. These windows were often replaced at the New Year and at that time formed a natural setting for the most popular form of papercut, 'window flowers'. Small in size and always red, the colour of joy, these were pasted onto the inside of the paper windows transforming the room by day and at night, when the lamp was lit, adding to the gaiety of the street. The lamp was also decorated with papercuts which no doubt danced in the flickering light.

In the Sung Dynasty one of the oldest and most popular forms of entertainment was the shadow theatre which was the translation of the 'window flowers' into movement and action. In this theatre the flat puppet is held between the source of light and a white screen onto which the shadow of the puppet is cast. The puppet is made of animal skin and is cut and coloured in much the same fashion as a papercut (Fig. 2).

Although windows were the most effective place for papercuts, they also hung from the lintels of doorways like lace curtains. Walls, ceilings and pillars were likewise decorated as were a mass of smaller objects — candles, cakes, the corners of mirrors, furniture and gift boxes. The technique finds its equivalent in metal, leather and cotton appliqué crafts, as well as in lacquer ware decoration where cut paper stencils are frequently used.

Weddings, birthdays, local festivals and celebrations all found a use for these papercuts which are known as 'happy flowers'. But it was the widespread practice of silk embroidery that sustained a regular demand. Sericulture originated in China over three thousand years ago and the tradition of embroidery is both very long and highly developed. Papercuts were made in endless varieties to satisfy a vast market. A white papercut of the desired size, shape and design is pasted or sewn onto the silk to be embroidered. This is done over the papercut in a free choice of colours. Designs for pockets, shoes, sleeves and waistcoats were sold in pairs while others for children's caps, men's tobacco pouches, pillows, cushions and table cloths all conveying subtle, charming and appropriate good wishes, were readily available.

Giant papercuts were made as stencils for a different process of textile decoration in the production of indigo blue and white cotton. This ancient craft goes back to even before the T'ang Dynasty and the designs are almost identical to those of papercuts. A very stiff paper coated with persimmon oil serves as a stencil and is placed over the undyed cloth. A mixture of lime and bean flour is applied through the cut patterns of the stencil onto the cloth beneath. This paste acts as a resist as the cloth is dipped in indigo dye and when it is scraped off, the design is revealed in brilliant white against the rich indigo blue background (Fig. 3).

The technique of the papercut has also been used in decorating pottery, the earliest example so far found being the glazed wares of the T'ang period. In these and in later blue and white village porcelain, a papercut is dipped into the coloured oxide and applied to the pottery before it is fired. In this way repetitive effects can be obtained with a wonderful economy of means (Fig. 4).

During the decline and disruption of traditional life in the Ch'ing Dynasty (1644-1912), folk crafts inevitably suffered, but during the last thirty years there has been a revival of interest particularly in papercuts. In 1940 the Lu Hsun Art Academy in Yenan drew attention to the skill and beauty of the papercuts it had collected from the north-west provinces. Members of the Academy and the Peking Central Institute of Fine Art succeeded in mastering the craft and bringing to it new themes. The government also came to the rescue and the most gifted of the surviving folk artists were employed as teachers.

Today the press of China makes great use of the visual effects of papercuts to decorate its pages and since 1950, this ancient craft which had been so poorly documented in the past, has become the subject of many books. Graphic artists both in China and abroad have come to appreciate the direct appeal and design qualities of the technique and to learn from it. At the same time new subject matter is being introduced. The vast quantities of papercuts now required both at home and for export have necessitated refinements in production involving the use of precut stencils to ensure perfectly uniform results. While the new papercuts of China may lack the inspiration of folk art, they do demonstrate the continued importance of an ancient craft in a modern society.

Fig. 1 Earliest known papercut discovered in Sinkiang
圖版 1 在新疆出土的最早期的剪紙

Fig. 2 Shadow puppet of a girl playing with a ball
圖版 2 少女玩球的皮影

Fig. 3　Indigo print with a phoenix and peony design
圖版 3　印有鳳凰牡丹圖案的靛藍印花布

Fig. 4　Village blue and white bowl with stencilled design
圖版 4　用剪紙印上圖案的農村釉下青花陶碗

Chinese Symbolism

In sharp contrast to a refined art which is an expression of an artist's individuality, usually motivated by the quest for personal fame, folk art is the result of the collective experience of a people. From the beginning of Chinese civilization to the present, folk art traditions have been transmitted from generation to generation. Embodied within the tradition is a 'collective memory' not only of art forms but also of the symbolic, mythological and legendary content of the great number of subjects depicted.

The folk artist uses subjects with which he is most familiar and his adoption of plant life in all its varieties is the most characteristic. Flowers and plants of every kind appear in his art and they carry both aesthetic and symbolic values, the two elements enhancing each other in the overall effect. The lotus that emerges miraculously quite perfect from the depths of muddy water and which is consequently the symbol of purity, is a well known example. The lotus is also the flower which represents one of the four seasons, summer. The others are prunus, which is symbolic of beauty, for winter; peony, symbolic of wealth, for spring; and the chrysanthemum, symbolic of endurance, for autumn.

However important plants have become as emblems in the course of time, the animals which surround and serve the farmer are of no less significance. The buffalo, goat, rabbit and pig all have sacrificial functions while mandarin ducks, depicted swimming in pairs, (often among lotuses) are emblematic of marital bliss. Long before the Christian era, animals together with the mythical dragon, had been canalized into the twelve cyclical animals of the Chinese calendar. The twelve are the rat, ox, tiger, rabbit, dragon, snake, horse, goat, monkey, cock, dog and pig. The present cycle began with the year of the rat in 1972 and finishes in 1983, the year of the pig.

The dragon introduces a supernatural element and it is the first of the four spiritually endowed creatures with a very special and ancient place in Chinese symbolism and mythology. It is not the gruesome monster of medieval imagination, but is emblematic of the spirit of change and therefore of life itself. The Chinese willingly believe in this divine, beneficent and mysterious creature; it features in their ancient history, legends of Buddhism abound with it, Taoist tales tell of its doings, and the whole country-side is filled with folk stories of its hidden abodes which none dare disturb.

The dragon is often depicted alone or in pairs chasing a pearl, one of the eight precious objects, and also with its female counterpart, the mythical phoenix, which is similar in appearance to the peacock and pheasant. When depicted alone the phoenix, which is the second of the supernatural creatures, is symbolic of feminine beauty. Together with the dragon they are emblematic of the perfect marriage.

The third of the supernatural creatures is the mythical *ch'i-lin* sometimes described as a unicorn. It is very well mannered and radiates perfect goodwill, gentleness and benevolence to all living creatures. Its appearance in no matter what circumstances can only be a very good omen (No. 6, p. 41). The fourth and last is the tortoise which, though seldom depicted, is a symbol of long life, strength and endurance.

By surrounding themselves with images rich in symbolic meanings and living in an atmosphere created by them, the Chinese hope that the sentiments expressed will be granted. These sentiments take the form of wishes; for good luck, a long life, male heirs, health, wealth and worldly honours. The images represent a comprehensive insurance scheme for this world and the next. The mere representation of an object may be enough to convey a wish; a stag, pine or crane would symbolise a long life; a coin or ingot, wealth etc. But in order to hide the banality of the wishes represented in this way, several symbolic elements are often combined together in subtle and elaborate compositions. For example the 'three friends' are represented by the plum, pine and bamboo, which together symbolise resolution, loyalty and dignity the qualities of a gentleman, while the 'three blessings' (good fortune, long life and many sons) are represented by combining the Buddha's hand citrus, the peach and the pomegranate into one design (No. 3, p. 39).

Combinations of more than one symbolic representation are also derived from language. Chinese is monosyllabic with no articles, endings or sex distinctions. With only a limited number of available sounds it is a language unusually rich in double and treble meanings and humour based on the play on words which have the same sound. A simple example is the word fish 魚 (*yu*) which has the same sound in Chinese as the word for abundance 餘 (*yu*)(No. 53, p. 85). But these puns are seldom simple and in fact even the Chinese themselves may find the meaning and symbolism of involved subjects difficult to understand. For example, a picture of a grasshopper sitting on top of its cage may not immediately bring to mind a high ranking government official. Its name 蟈蟈兒 (*kuo kuo erh*) sounds very similar in mandarin to an official 官兒 (*kuan erh*). Because it sits outside the cage it symbolises the attainment of a high rank, the ultimate aim of so many civil servants.

A wish is frequently enforced with a written character or group of characters, beautifully adaptable for papercut designs. The character 喜 (happiness) is frequently doubled (No. 126, p. 137; No. 147, p. 156) and others may be modified in shape to emphasise their meaning.

Buddhism and Taoism have provided Chinese art with the strongest inspiration with its concepts of the 'Immortals' and the part serious, part burlesque accounts of their miraculous deeds. From this great and unclassifiable pantheon it is sufficient to mention Shou-lao, the God of Long Life and the Eight Immortals. Shou-lao is a friendly old man with a long beard and a lofty brow who carries a gnarled stick and a peach and is accompanied by a deer or a crane. The Eight Immortals, who are often depicted with Shou-lao are Li Tieh-kuai, who carries an iron crutch and is the patron of the sick; Chung-li Ch'uan carries a fan with which he can raise the dead; Lan Ts'ai-ho carries a basket and is the protector of horticulture; Chang Kuo-lao rides a mule and is the patron of old men; Ho Hsien-ku carries a lotus blossom and is the patroness of housewives; Lu Tung-pin carries a flywisk and is honoured as a scholar; Han Hsiang-tzu carries a flute and is the patron deity of musicians and lastly Ts'ao Kuo-ch'iu who carries castanets, is the patron diety of actors. The representation of figures in papercuts is particularly difficult but Chang Kuo-lao and Li Tieh-kuai (Nos. 65, 66 on pp. 92, 93) are part of a lively and unconventional set from Hupei.

Other characters from famous plays, folk tales and operas have been immortalised in the popular art of today in which the achievements of the new society are also being incorporated into a new mythology. Children playing table tennis recall the diplomatic significance of this game, and representations of 'the great leap forward' in papercuts can only bring the wish for progress and prosperity a step nearer to actuality.

Technique

No elaborate methods and daunting array of tools are required to produce papercuts which in China was essentially a folk art of the village, street and market. Its beauty lies in its uncomplicated and direct expression and in its delicate and refined execution.

The most important tool is a rectangular wooden tray which has a rim, about one centimetre in depth, running round its edge. Traditionally this tray is filled to the top of the rim with melted animal fat to which finely powdered charcoal has been added until it has a thick consistency. When this has cooled it provides a smooth, resilient working surface that can be used for years. Today a hard rubberized material could be substituted.

The knives consist of extremely sharp blades secured between two fine slivers of bamboo bound together with cloth and string. The remaining tools are sharpening stones, sharp pointed scissors, a pair of metal tweezers, pins, a bag of flour and a broad flat knife to smooth the surface of the board after cutting.

For an original design a drawing is first made with Chinese ink and brush. Ten to twenty sheets of thin paper are placed on the cutting board which has been dusted with flour to prevent any adhesion, with the design on top of the pile. The best paper used for making papercuts is *hsuan* or *yu k'ou* paper from Ningkuo in South Anhwei, which is extremely thin, strong and absorbent. Paper pins

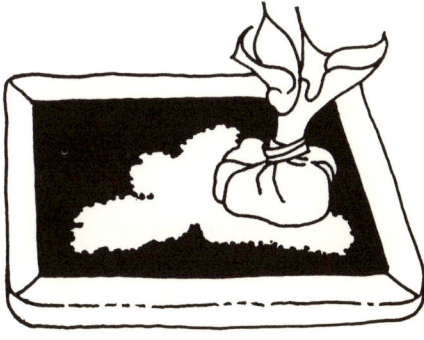

are driven through the sheets of paper to fasten these together. The paper can also be sewn together and fixed to the cutting board with pins as it is essential for the sheets to remain in position during cutting. These are kept flat with the left hand while the cutting knife, held upright in the right, follows the lines of the design penetrating through the paper to the board below. A pin is used to remove the unwanted sections of the design and when completed, the papercuts are lifted with the tweezers.

Using this basic technique many regional styles and variations have developed throughout China. Whereas most 'window flowers' would be of a size, shape and transparency suitable for a window, papercuts can vary enormously in size from a tiny cake decoration to a huge adornment, made in sections, for a ceiling. Papercuts designed as decorations for lacquer from Chuanchou in Fukien differ from those made in the silk district of Kiangsu for embroidery patterns. The Wei County of Hopei specialises in theatrical subjects while Chekiang produces white filigree patterns of incredible delicacy. In contrast the western provinces, Shensi and Shansi produce paper forms which are extremely powerful, simple and direct and which in recent years have had a considerable influence on Chinese graphic art.

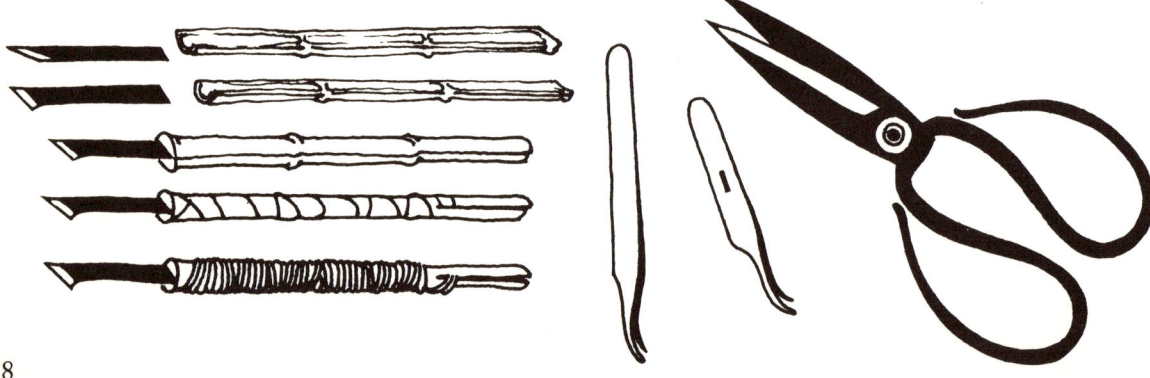

From these varieties there are two prevailing styles of cutting. The simplest, which consists of cutting away thin lines within large solid areas of paper, creates designs which are bold and strong (Shensi and Shansi) (No. 49, p. 80). The second style, in which the design is formed by a tracery of thin paper lines with large spaces between cut away, produces extremely delicate and refined results (Hopei and Chekiang) (No. 128, p. 139). In both methods the completed design must 'hang together', a discipline which gives to the papercut its unique design qualities. In some cases the two methods are combined with great effect.

Apart from the simple monochrome papercuts there are those which combine a number of coloured papers. In one type individual parts of the design are cut out of different coloured papers which are assembled together into a papercut collage. In another colourful variation which is one unique speciality of Foshan in Kwangtung Province, the 'lines' of the papercut are made from a single piece of metal foil paper and this is backed by different coloured papers which emphasise the various parts of the design (Nos. 172-176, p. 175).

It is, however, the application of transparent dyes to the actual thin white papercuts which produces the most subtle coloured effects (Nos. 7-14, pp. 42, 43). This has been perfected particularly in Hopei where the coloured dyes are added to the slightly damp pile of papercuts and allowed to penetrate through. The different dyes used also diffuse into each other and the effect becomes wonderfully muted when placed on a transluscent paper window.

Papercuts are also made with pointed scissors and the design is frequently and miraculously cut without any form of guide line. They are usually simpler and larger than those made with a knife and only one or two can be made at the same time.

The common technique of producing repetitive symmetrical shapes by folding the paper before cutting which is known to all school children throughout the world, is not widely used in China. This is probably because free natural forms are more frequently used in designs than abstract shapes.

Until recent times it was fairly common for the excellence of a young girl's papercuts to be judged by a bride-groom's family before marriage. In Chekiang and Shantung where the craft was learnt from childhood it had the same importance as embroidery and cooking. Throughout China the craft has traditionally been in the hands of peasant women who organised families into work groups to satisfy the constant demand for embroidery patterns and the special requirements of weddings, funerals and New Year celebrations.

It was also at this time of year that individual professional craftsmen, who devoted their lives to the perfection of their art, would appear in the street markets of China (Figs. 5-8, pp. 30-33). These craftsmen had no status and no security but they provided a seasonal art which transformed bleak interiors, added festivity to the streets and brought the essential good wishes to millions of Chinese. It is on two levels that their folk art can now be appreciated; as the embodiment of a popular mythology and also as the essence of a pictorial tradition.

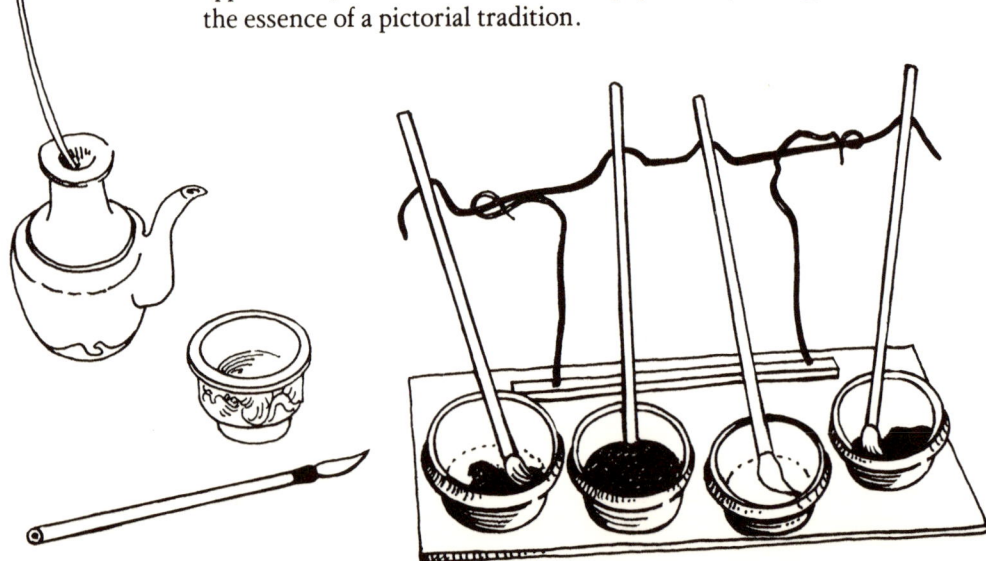

創造與利用

　　大約在公元一世紀，中國人發明了韌度最強和用途最廣的材料——紙。此後幾百年間紙大概依然被看作寶貴的甚至是稀世珍品，它的日常及裝飾用途就受到嚴重的限制。

　　一九五九年，在新疆于田縣塔里木盆地以南一個古城的考古地區，發現了玫瑰花形的剪紙（見11頁，圖版１）。這個地區使用剪紙可上溯至南北朝時代（公元三八六至五八一），那時，剪紙可能用作漆器裝飾和建築物的設計圖案。靛藍襯白色的布塊碎片也有發現。

　　早期的剪紙看來不可能是圖案與圖畫的作品，而可能是表示吉祥的中國文字。據「酉陽雜俎」所載：「北朝婦人，常以立春日進春書」，從此可見，北朝婦女習慣在立春日把「宜春帖子」又名「春書」的剪紙掛在門楣上。

　　在唐朝（公元六一八至九○六），詩人崔道融有詩：「欲剪宜春字，春寒入剪刀」。而在同一時期從其他資料中獲知剪紙是用於裝飾植物；另有剪成蝴蝶形的和剪成花卉形的，是給婦女戴在頭上的。剪紙也用於食物的裝飾，特別是用於餅食的裝飾，以便人們在重陽節携往登高。南宋（一一二七至一二七九）「東京夢華錄」謂：「唐時都人出郭登高，各以粉麪蒸糕，上插剪綵小旗」。在十三世紀，周密著的「志雅堂雜鈔」記有一古癖少年，他在自己的外衣的長袖上剪出文字和花的圖案。

　　剪紙的用途到了這一時期肯定已很廣泛，而剪紙的主題內容已經在神話故事的，歷史的和戲劇的人物以及佛道二教的象徵圖案以外再加上了動物、雀鳥和花草。

　　二十多年以前，中國的大部份窗戶都像一千多年以前那樣，還是用紙來糊裱。這些紙糊裱在窗格子上，乾了就會變得綳緊。每逢新年佳節，這些窗戶在換上新紙後再加上剪紙，即所謂「窗花」。這些剪紙，體積很小通常呈紅色，表示喜慶，貼在紙糊的窗戶內，使人在日夜間看起來都有煥然一新之感。燈光一着，街道上就更加充滿歡樂的氣氛了。燈盞也用剪紙來裝飾，確是閃閃生輝。

　　宋朝最古老和最流行的娛樂節目之一是皮影戲。這種有動作的皮影戲是從「窗花」演變而成的。戲中的扁平傀儡被支撐在燈光與一塊白幕之間來加以操縱，這樣傀儡的影子就會活現在幕上。傀儡是用動物的皮做成的，其剪切與着色的方法與剪紙大同小異（見11頁，圖版２）。

　　雖然窗戶是最能發揮剪紙功效的地方，門楣上也掛有剪紙，看起來像通花簾子似的。一如許多較細小的東西，像蠟燭、餅食、鏡角、像具和禮盒那樣，牆壁、天花板和柱子上也有類似的裝飾。在金屬、皮革和棉布的鑲飾工藝中，剪切和應用

的是同一方法，而在漆器的裝飾中，硬紙製成的鏤花模板是經常被採用的。

那稱為「喜花」的剪紙，在婚禮、生日和喜慶節日都可派用場。但維持對剪紙的一個經常需求的是絲繡的廣泛流行。蠶絲業遠在三千多年以前始創於中國，這種刺繡，傳統悠久，發展高速。剪紙成品以其數之不盡的式樣來滿足廣大市場的需要。刺繡時把一張選定尺寸、形狀和圖案的白色剪紙貼上或縫上備作刺繡用的絲布上，然後用彩線將花紋繡在剪紙上。為口袋、鞋面、袖子和背心而設計的剪紙在市面上成雙成對地出售，其他的還有童帽子、男士的煙草袋、枕頭、墊子和桌布等物用的剪紙圖案，都別具精工和吸引力，此外，更有含有各種好意頭的剪紙任君選擇。

用硬紙製成的巨型鏤花模板是給紡織品作印花用的，以便出產靛藍印花布。這個古老工藝可上溯至唐朝甚至唐以前，所用的圖案與剪紙的幾乎完全相同。將一塊塗有柿油作印花用的鏤花模板覆蓋在待染的布面上，再把石灰與豆粉製成的防染劑刮印在模板的鏤花上而使該防染劑依圖案之規劃往下滲至白布面上。這種防染劑在布下浸靛藍染缸的時候起防染的作用，刮掉這一層防染劑，整個靛藍底白面的圖案就會耀眼生輝地顯現出來（見12頁，圖版3）。

剪紙的技術也用於陶器的裝飾，被發現的最早期例証是唐朝的彩釉陶器。這些陶器和後期的農村釉下靑花陶器，是用剪紙上鈷釉，印在陶器面上再用火燒。用這種方法和最節省的花費就可得到重複圖案的效果（見12頁，圖版4）。

傳統生活在清朝（一六四四至一九一二）陷於衰落和瓦解，民間工藝趨於式微，但在最近的三十年間人們對民間工藝，特別是對剪紙的愛好又告復興起來。一九四〇年延安魯迅藝術學院對收集自西北各省的剪紙的技巧和美觀很重視。這個學院和北京中央美術學院的學員們都對這種工藝加以精研，並且還注入了新的題材。政府也對民間工藝進行挽救，最有天才的老藝人都獲聘為教師。

今天，中國的出版界正大規模利用剪紙的圖案和裝飾效果，來裝飾書頁，而且，自從一九五〇年以來，這個過去在文獻紀錄中稀見的古代工藝，已經成為許多著作的論述主題了。國內外的圖象藝術家都對這種技術的直接感染力和圖案的特質備加讚賞，都來學習這種技術。同時，這種工藝也採納了新的題材內容，而且，國內市場和出口目前對剪紙的大量需求，已經使這種產品的製模工作日趨完美和達到一致的效果。雖然缺乏民間藝術的靈感，新的中國剪紙都能証明古代工藝在現代社會仍然是重要的。

中國象徵主義

　　與往往表現藝術家的個性、通常以追求個人名譽為動機的精美藝術成強烈的對照，民間藝術是集體經驗的成果。從中國文化的開端到現今，民間藝術的傳統就代代相傳下來。體現在這個傳統中不僅是藝術形象的「集體記憶」，也是象徵主義的、神話的和傳說的內容的「集體記憶」。

　　民間藝術家所描寫的大都是他熟悉的題材，他對所有各種植物的採用是最具特色的。各種花卉和植物都出現在他的藝術作品中，這些花卉和植物兼有美觀的和象徵主義的價值，這兩個因素，於全面效果上看，可說是牡丹綠葉，相得益彰。那出於污泥而不染的蓮，必然是純潔的象徵，這是大家都知道的一個例子。蓮也是代表四季之一的夏季的花。此外還有梅，美麗的象徵，代表冬季；牡丹，富有象徵，代表春季；菊，堅忍不拔的象徵，代表秋季。

　　不管植物在中國象徵主義中是怎樣重要，那些對農民有用的動物亦有同樣的重要性。牛、羊、兔和豬都可作獻祭之用，成雙成對（常在蓮叢中穿梭）的戲水鴛鴦則是婚姻至樂的象徵。早在耶穌紀元以前，人們已把一些動物和龍配在一起而作為中國曆法的十二生肖。這十二生肖是鼠、牛、虎、兔、龍、蛇、馬、羊、猴、雞、狗和豬。現在的周期始於鼠年，一九七二年；終於豬年，一九八三年。

　　龍具有一個超自然的因素，因為牠是中國的象徵主義和神話中佔有十分特殊和古老地位的四靈的為首一個。牠不是中世紀想像的可怕怪物，而是變幻的象徵，所以也是人生的象徵。中國人會樂意地信仰這個神聖的、慈善為懷的和神奇莫測的生物；牠是中國古代歷史的一個特色，佛教傳說中的龍是多姿多采的，道教傳說也載有龍的各種活動，中國農村到處都流行着有關於龍的民間故事，在龍的隱居之所是任何人物都不敢干擾的。

　　龍常常被描繪成獨個兒或成雙成對追逐一顆珠——八寶之一。此外，陪着龍的也有作為雌性配偶的鳳，這種鳳跟孔雀和雉的外表相彷彿。當鳳，這個四靈中的第二個生物在作品中單獨出現的時候，是象徵女性的美麗。龍鳳一雙則是美滿婚姻的象徵。

　　四靈中的第三個生物是有時被描繪成身形似獨角獸的麒麟。麒麟不論在什麼環境中出現都是一個吉祥的預兆。（見41頁，圖6）。龜是四靈中的最後一個生物，龜被描繪的甚少，是長壽、力量和堅忍不拔的象徵。

　　用富於象徵的意義的畫像來圍繞着他們，中國人希望這些畫像所表示的心願能夠實現。他們的心願包括好運、長壽、有子為後嗣、健康、財富和世上的榮譽等。這些畫像不但可保

佑今世，而且可保佑來生。僅以一物就可代表一個願望；一頭鹿，一棵松或一隻鶴都可以單獨作爲長壽的象徵，一錢或一錠是代表財富，等等。但爲了掩飾因這樣而造成的平凡表現，幾個象徵主義的成份常常巧妙地結合在一起。例如，松竹梅代表「歲寒三友」，三者合而爲一表示一個男士的品格、堅毅、忠誠和威武不屈。而佛手、仙桃和石榴在同一圖案中則代表有福、長壽和多男子的「三大福佑」（見39頁，圖3）。

中國語言亦可作象徵主義的表現。中國語言是沒有冠詞、詞尾和性別的單音語。只憑藉爲數有限的，可用的聲音，這種語言一字雙義或三義的情形特別多，而其同音相諧而成的雙關語也極富幽默感。「魚」字是個簡單的例子，它跟「餘」同音，表示「有餘」（見85頁，圖53）。但這些雙關語很少是這麼簡單易懂的。事實上，就連中國人自己面對這些問題，也不容易找出它們所象徵的是什麼意思。例如，在一幅畫中有一隻蚱蜢坐在籠外的頂上，這就不能使人立即想到所指的是一個高級政府官員。蚱蜢又名「蟈蟈兒」跟國語的「官兒」同音。因爲是坐在籠子的外頭，這就象徵高級的官階，也就是許多文職官員的最遠大的目標。

很多時剪紙藝人用一個字或字組來配合剪紙的圖案。「喜」字常常雙寫（137頁，圖126；156頁，圖147），其他的字可用改變形體的方法來強調其意義。

佛教和道教的「衆神」和他們的既莊嚴又滑稽的事蹟給了中國藝術豐富的靈感。從這個數不盡和難分派別的衆神中提到壽老和八仙也就是夠的了。壽老是一位留着長長的鬍子和雙眉高高豎起的友善的老人，他隨身携帶的是木瘤橫生的拐杖和桃子，跟着他的是一頭鹿和一隻鶴。與壽老一起在圖中出現的是拿着鐵拐杖的病人庇護者李鐵拐；手中的扇可以把死人扇活的鍾離權；手持一個籃子的園藝業庇護者藍采和；騎驟的老人庇護者張果老；手持蓮花的家庭主婦庇護者何仙姑；手執飛鞭有學者之尊榮的呂洞賓；有長笛在手的樂師庇護者韓湘子，最後一個是拿着响板的演員庇護者曹國舅。用剪紙來表現人物的形像是特別困難的，但在來自湖北省那組不落陳套而又栩栩如生的剪紙中就有張果老和李鐵拐的形像（見92、93頁，圖65、66）。

來自著名戲劇、民間故事和歌劇的其他人物都已成爲今天民間藝術作品中的不朽形像，在這種民間藝術中，新社會的成就也被編入新的神話裏。小童打乒乓球使人回想起這種遊戲在外交上的重要性，而在剪紙中所表現的「大躍進」是希望進步與繁榮能早日現實。

剪紙的技巧

剪紙的製作，無需精心巧設的方法，也不用洋洋大觀的工具。剪紙在中國基本上是鄉村、街頭和市集的民間工藝。這種工藝的美表現在它的簡樸和明快的表達方式上，也表現在它的細緻和精煉的技巧上。

最重要的工具是一個長方形的、用來將畫稿和紙疊放在上面刻製的油盤。油盤的四周圍着一條高約一公分的欄邊，欄邊內全盤依傳統辦法塡滿加有炭粉的動物油脂。冷却後盤面就變成平滑和有彈性，可供多年工作之用。今天，硬膠料可取而代之。

所用的刀是夾在兩片薄竹之間用布條子包起來再用棉線或繩子拴牢。其他的工具是磨刀石、尖銳的剪子、一把小鉗子、針、粉袋和一把用來刮平工作後的油盤面的撥刀。

在設計一張新畫稿時，需要首先用筆墨在紙上繪畫出一個圖案。刻前在油盤上面舖上十至二十張薄紙，而畫稿是置於紙疊的頂上的。這油盤面上已事先印上粉末以防畫稿和紙疊黏在油盤上，剪或刻紙所用的紙最好的是產自安徽南部寧國的宣紙或玉扣紙，這種紙最薄、最韌和最具吸收能力。紙疊可用紙唸扣緊在一起，亦可以用針綫把紙張縫牢，然後用針把紙疊釘在油盤上，因爲在進行刻製的時候，紙張一定要保留在固定位置上。刻紙時左手按盤，右手以垂直的角度持刻刀，依照畫稿的綫路插穿紙疊直透至油盤。圖案中不用的部份則可用一根針挑去。剪紙完成後可用一把小鉗子把製成的剪紙從油盤上鉗上來。（剪紙工具，見17、18、20、21頁）

中國許多地區的不同風格和變化的剪紙，是用這個基本技術而造成的。各種「窗花」都可說是同一大小、形體和透明度而適宜於裝飾窗戶，但剪紙的大小却可以由小小的餅糕裝飾擴大至巨大的組合式天花板裝飾。產自福建泉州的剪紙是爲漆器裝飾而設計的，而產自江蘇的絲綢區的剪紙則是爲刺繡圖案而設計的，兩者各不相同。河北省蔚縣專門製作戲劇題材的剪紙，而浙江省則出產極具雅緻精細的圖案，在對照之下，西部的陝西和山西兩省所產的剪紙顯得極具功力，簡樸又明快，已對近幾年來的中國圖象藝術產生重要的影响。

剪紙技巧分爲陰刻和陽刻兩種。最簡易的製法是陰刻，陰刻剪紙刻去纖細綫條，使餘下未刻的地方構成鮮明而簡樸的圖案（陝西和山西）（見80頁，圖49）。第二種方法是陽刻，這是將大部份的地方刻去，圖案由餘下的幼綫紋構成，這樣就得到極其細緻和精巧的效果（河北和浙江）（見139頁，圖128）。不論採用的是那一種方法，所完成的圖案的各部份必須是連在一起的，這是構成剪紙獨特性質的一個必須奉行的准則。有時候以上兩法並用會產生很精彩的效果。

除了單色的剪紙之外，還有由多種顏色的紙組合而成的剪紙。同是一個圖案可由不同顏色的紙裁出各個部份，然後將各個部份拼貼起來成一張拼貼圖案的剪紙。廣東佛山的剪紙獨有其多姿多彩的變化，這種剪紙的圖案輪廓是由一張錫紙造成的，以不同顏色的紙作爲襯底，對圖案的各個部份起強調的作用（見175頁，圖 172-176 ）。

　　透明色彩加上又薄又白的剪紙上可產生最精巧的色澤效果（見 42、43 頁，圖 7-14 ）。河北省在這方面的工作特別完善，即把色彩加在微濕的紙疊上，讓它往下滲透。所用的不同色彩相互混合在一起，貼在半透明的紙窗上就能產生色澤柔和的美感。

　　剪紙也可用尖銳的剪刀來製造，而且不需要依照任何指示格式也能剪出神奇美妙的圖案。這些圖案通常比用刀刻出來的較爲簡單和粗大。而且，在同一時間只能剪出一張或兩張。全世界學童都知道用先摺紙而後剪出重覆而對稱的圖案的普通技術，但這個技術在中國並未得到廣泛的採用。這可能是因爲那無拘束的自然形象比抽象的形狀較常用作剪紙圖案的緣故。

　　在結婚前，坤宅閨秀的剪紙擅長要經乾宅的人作一番品評，這種風氣直至近代還是相當普遍。在浙江和山東兩省，這種工藝的研習是從童年開始的，它跟刺繡和烹飪同樣重要。全中國的剪紙工藝都已因襲地操在農婦的手中，她們把各家婦女組成工作組，以滿足刺繡圖案的經常需求和婚、喪、新年喜慶的特別需求。

　　那些畢生致力於藝術的獨立職業剪紙藝人，亦在新年時間在中國的街頭擺設檔口。這些工藝人既沒有社會地位，也沒有安全的保障，但他們所提供的應節藝術品，却可改善室內的沉悶色調，使街上充滿節日的歡慶氣氛和帶給千千萬萬中國人共同必需的祝願。

　　這些民間藝術作品，現在受到大衆欣賞，是因爲它們含有家喻戶曉的神話內容和傳統圖畫的精粹。

Figs. 5-8　Papercut craftsman at work in the streets of Peking, 1935

圖版 5-8　一位剪紙藝人在北京街頭工作，攝於一九三五年。

8

河北　Hopei
北京　Peking
蔚縣　Weihsien
天津　Tientsin

北京
Peking

1
Dragon Dance
The dragon, symbol of creative power, has the ability to change its size and shape and even to disappear altogether. Different varieties of the creature support the abodes of the gods, create wind and rain, rule over springs and rivers and guard hidden treasure. Here its effigy is held aloft as it is playfully taunted by a ball representing a flaming pearl.

1
舞龍
龍，創造能力的象徵，具有改變自身體積、形狀甚至隱身於無形的本領。各種不同的龍可分別保護眾神的居所、呼風喚雨、統轄源流江河和護衛大地蘊藏的財富。這裏所見是龍的紮像被高高舉起，而代表紅焰之珠的一個繡球正對它百般戲弄。

2
Bottle Gourd
As it grows everywhere in China and is such a useful tool and container when it is dried, something of a cult has grown up around the gourd. It has many associations with fertility and magic and according to Taoist belief contains a secret miracle drug, the elixir of immortality.

2
葫蘆
因為葫蘆在中國到處蔓生，去掉爪瓤曬乾後又是現成的一種工具和盛器，所以，葫蘆逐漸成為被人尊崇的一種東西。由葫蘆可以產生與家肥屋潤和魔法有關的許多聯想，而且，道家相信，葫蘆內藏有仙丹。

3
Basket of Fruit with Flowers
The three fruit represented are a Buddha's hand citrus 佛手 (*fo shou*), a peach and a pomegranate. Together they convey the wish 'good fortune, long life, and many noble sons' 多福多壽多男子 (*to fu, to shou, to nan tze*), the Buddha's hand citrus being used homonymously for good fortune 福 (*fu*), the peach being symbolic of long life and the pomegranate, because of its numerous seeds, symbolic of many children.

3

多福多壽多男子
籃內的三種別具象徵的鮮果是佛手、仙桃和石榴。這些鮮果擺在一起，是傳達「多福多壽多男子」的希望。佛手被一致地用來象徵「多福」，而仙桃則是「長壽」之意，石榴多籽，表示「多得男子」。

4
Chrysanthemum
Because of its ability to withstand cold weather this flower is a symbol of endurance. The design is an embroidery pattern for a lady's shoe.

5
Peony
The gorgeous colouring and full blossom of this flower has made it the symbol or riches and nobility. This design is an embroidery pattern for the neck-piece of a lady's waistcoat.

4
菊肥霜艷繡紅鞋
因爲有經受得住寒冷天氣的能力，菊花是堅忍不拔的象徵。這是給女子鞋面設計的一個刺繡圖案。

5
牡丹開花，富貴榮華
因爲牡丹色彩燦爛，花容茂盛，故成爲富有與高貴的象徵。這是女裝背心領邊的一個刺繡圖案。

**6
Ch'i-lin**
One of the four spiritually endowed creatures, the elegant light-footed *Ch'i-lin* does not tread on any living thing. Represented with a boy 貴子 (*kwei tze*) holding a lotus flower 蓮 (*lien*) and a reed organ 笙 (*sheng*), the picture is associated with the bedroom, bringing wishes for a succession of noble sons 連生貴子 (*lien sheng kwei tze*).

**6
麒麟送子**
麒麟是四靈之，牠是不踩踏生物的。以一個男孩手持蓮花和笙作爲聯想，這一張剪紙是貼在寢室裏用的，象徵連生貴子。

蔚縣
Weihsien

7

8

9

10

7-10
Opera Masks

11-14
Theatrical Characters

7-10
京劇臉譜

11-14
戲劇人物

11

12

13

14

天津
Tientsin

15
Candlesticks
Designed to be pasted on pillars etc., these papercuts follow the form of candlesticks which stand on the family altar. They carry a variety of wishes. From bottom to top on the small pair these are; a coin design, the character for happiness 喜 (*hsi*) doubled, a lotus (purity), the endless knot (a long life), an ingot (prosperity), and finally the four characters 'peace on earth' on the candles. Just above the base of the larger candlestick a pair of *ju-i* have been added — curve shaped sceptres which ensure the fulfillment of all the wishes represented.

15
燭臺雙喜，萬事如意
這些剪紙是貼在柱子等地方的，剪成家庭神台上的燭臺樣式。它們都表達出各種希望。較小一對由底部至頂部依次是一個錢幣、喜字雙立，表示雙喜、蓮花象徵純潔、無窮盡的環節有長壽之意、錠則祈願繁榮昌盛，最後，在蠟燭上的四個字是「天下太平」。在較大的一對燭臺的底座上方置有一對如意，是要保證各種象徵的願望全部都能實現。

16
Pendant
A magic bowl contains an ingot representing prosperity. The two leaves symbolise bliss.

17
Pendant
The messengers of the God of Wealth knock on the door of the house. Strings of coins are on the roof above. The chrysanthemum, symbol of endurance, gives a lasting significance to this wish for riches.

18
Pendant
The character for good fortune 福 (*fu*) is set in a lace-like pendant designed to hang from the lintel of a door and float like a curtain. Again the chrysanthemum adds endurance to the wish.

16
聚寶盆
寶盆內有一錠，象徵繁榮昌盛。兩葉則表示天賜福樂。

17
財神叫門
財神的使者在敲門。錢繩繞在屋頂上。象徵堅忍的菊花，含有永久保留財富的願望。

18
天賜福樂
這張綴以福字的通花吊錢，從門楣垂下，飄動起來像一堂簾子。再加上菊花，含有長久保留福樂的願望。

17

18

47

19
Pigs bearing Wealth
Perhaps because every part can be utilized the pig is a highly esteemed domestic and sacrificial animal. Its prolific breeding habits have inevitably inspired folk artists to burden the animal with symbols of wealth and prosperity.

20
Money Tree
The idea of a tree regularly bearing fruit in the form of ingots and coins has a direct and universal appeal. Here two boys, attendants of the God of Wealth, gather the harvest for distribution. The three characters on the magic bowl read 'one million gold'.

19
豬仔一胎又一胎，金銀財富滾滾來
或許因為每一部份都可被利用，豬是很受人看重和可供獻祭之用的一種家畜。牠的一胎可產成羣小豬的繁殖特性，早已必然地激勵民間藝術家把豬作為財富與繁榮的象徵。

20
搖錢樹
樹經常結出來的不是果子而是錠和圓形的錢幣，這個想象正切合普遍的要求。這裏所見是兩個小孩，財神的侍從，在收集錢幣以便分配。在寶盆上標着「百萬金」三個字。

百萬金

山東　Shantung

52 21

21
Flowers and Birds

22-24
Bonsai

21
花鳥知春

22-24
盆景

25
Magpies
Traditionally the calls of magpies, especially in the early morning, herald the arrival of good news or a visitor. The bird is therefore a messenger of joy and happiness.

26
Orchid
Because of its exquisite characteristics and numerous varieties, the orchid is emblematic of love and beauty and a symbol of fragrance and refinement.

25
喜鵲叫，客人到
傳說喜鵲鳴叫，尤其是在大清早，是預報好消息和客人到訪。因此，這種鳥就是傳遞喜樂信息的使者。

26
芬芳馥郁說芝蘭
因為蘭花有優美的特性，而且品種繁多，所以她是愛情、美麗、芬芳馥郁和幽雅的象徵。

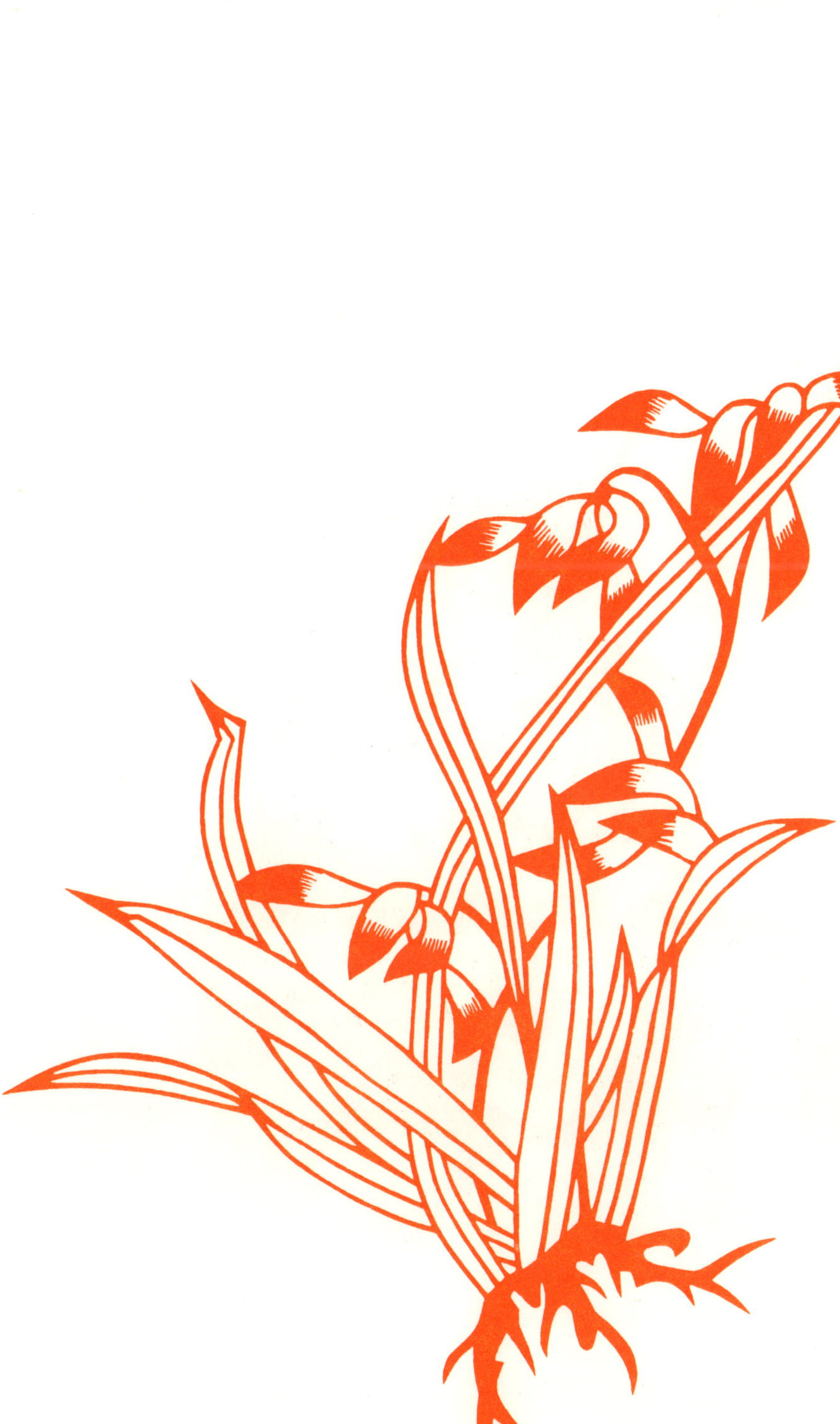

27
Girl riding a Donkey

27
騎驢的姑娘

**28
Lion**
The Buddhist guardian lion is a creature which resembles the old palace favourite, the Pekinese dog. It is common to find a pair of these diminuitive, playful animals in the role of guardians and the male usually holds a brocade ball with ribbons attached.

**28
獅子小小，滑稽可笑**
佛教的守護獅是跟深宮中的寵物北京狗相似的一種生物。這些小小的滑稽北京狗經常被人充當守護獅。雄的通常抓着結有緞帶的繡球。

山西　Shansi

29
Character from Mythology

29
神話中的人物

30
Character from Mythology

30
神話中的人物

31
Camel and Trader

31
駱駝與商人

32
Horsecart

32
馬車

33
Rooster
This splendid bird has many virtues and attributes. His crown is a mark of literary success, a pun on the Chinese for crown 冠 sounding the same as official 官. His spurs are proof of a fighting disposition and courage and yet he is considerate to hens and his time keeping is impeccable.

33
公雞
這種羽毛華麗奪目外表雄糾糾的公雞有很多優點和特徵。牠的冠從字面解是成功的標誌，又因爲讀音相同，「冠」字是「官」字的相關語。牠的雙距表現出十足的戰鬪格局和勇敢精神。不過，牠對母雞卻是體貼入微的，牠在報時方面的准確性是無懈可擊的。

34
Monkey Smoking

35
Monkey carrying Lanterns

34
吸旱煙的猴

35
挑燈籠的猴

陕西　Shensi
陕北　Northern Shensi
陕南　Southern Shensi

陝北

Northern Shensi

36
Pheasant
The golden pheasant shares many of the attributes of the phoenix being emblematic of beauty and good fortune. In the Ch'ing Dynasty it was the insignia on the court robes of civil officers of the second grade, while the silver pheasant was used by fifth grade civil officials.

36
雉雞
金雉具有許多與鳳凰相同的特徵，而鳳凰則是幸運和美麗的象徵。清朝二級文官的朝服是以金雉為徽章的，五級文官則用銀雉為朝服的徽章。

37
Dragon
Revered as one of the spiritually endowed creatures, the dragon is a blessing rather than a curse to man, with outstanding qualities, powers and heavenly connections. Perhaps for these reasons it was adopted by Chinese emperors as their personal emblem.

37
龍踞天子之尊
龍是四靈之一，牠超卓的氣質、超人的能力和與天庭的聯系，不但不降禍蒼生，而且還賜福人類。或許是為了這些緣故，龍就被中國皇帝用來作為他本人的象徵。

38
Tiger
The tiger is symbolic of courage and fierceness. In the Ch'ing Dynasty military officers of the fourth rank used its image as their insignia.

38
虎
虎是勇猛的象徵。清朝五級武官採用虎像作爲他們的徽章。

72

39
Mu Kwei-ying, a Theatrical Character
Pheasant feathers are an essential part of a warrior's headdress.

40, 41
Theatrical Characters

39
戲劇人物穆桂英
雉羽是戰士頭飾的基本部份。

40, 41
戲劇人物

42
A Hero from Mythology

43
Camel

42
神話中的一位英雄

43
駱駝

44, 45
The Monkey King and the Pig God
Characters from *The Journey to the West*

44, 45
孫悟空與豬八戒
「西遊記」中的人物。

75

陕南
Southern Shensi

46
Gathering Mulberry Leaves

46
探桑

47
Raising Chickens

47
養雞

48
Spinning

48
紡紗

49
Selling Firewood

50
Fisherman

49
賣柴

50
漁翁

51
Stag
As the stag is popularly believed to live to a great age it has become a symbol of long life and its horns when powdered and eaten can assist towards this end. In Chinese stag 鹿 (*lu*) is a pun on official income 祿 (*lu*).

51
鹿
因為人們一般地相信鹿可活到很高的年歲，所以，牠就成為長壽的象徵，而鹿角被磨成粉後之提供食用，有助於達致長壽的目的。「鹿」字是解作做官收入的「祿」字的相關語。

湖北　Hupei

52
Vase
In themselves, vases 瓶 (*ping*) are symbolic of peace 平 (*ping*). When the form of the vase is elongated the wish is for an enduring peace. A rounded form suggest the wish for a complete peace.

52
天下太平
瓶就是和平的象徵。長形的瓶所表示的願望是持久和平，而圓形所表示的則是十全十美的和平願望。

53
Fish and Lotus
This combination of a fish and a lotus carries the wish for successive years of abundance. Fish 魚 (*yu*) is a pun on abundance 餘 (*yu*) and lotus 蓮 (*lien*) on succession of 連 (*lien*).

53

連年有餘
魚和蓮含有「連年有餘」之意。「魚」是「餘」的相關語，「蓮」則是「連」的相關語。

**54
Magpie and Plum Blossom**
Magpies, heralds of joy and happiness, combined with plum blossom 梅 (*mei*) used here homonymously for brow 眉 (*mei*) carry the wish, 'may happiness radiate from your brow'.

**55
Pomegranate**
One of the 'three blessings', the pomegrante displaying many seeds symbolises numerous offspring.

54
喜上眉梢
喜鵲報喜，「梅」字與「眉」字同音，含有願君喜上眉梢之意。

55
榴開見子
石榴乃三大祝福之一，一榴多籽象徵百子千孫。

56
Phoenix and Peony
Revered as one of the four spiritually endowed creatures, the phoenix is symbolic of femininity and the chosen emblem of the Chinese empress. The peony represents wealth and nobility.

56
鳳戲牡丹
被作為四靈之一來崇拜,鳳凰是女子氣質和中國皇后的象徵。牡丹是富貴榮華的象徵。

**57
Boy and Lotus**
The lotus 蓮 (*lien*) is homonymously used here for succession 連 (*lien*). The boy represents noble offspring and combined they carry the wish for a succession of noble sons.

**57
連生貴子**
這兒「蓮」用作「連」是同音的關係。而孩子則代表高貴的子孫。「子」與「蓮」合用就有連生貴子的意願。

58
Fish and Lotus
The fish 魚 (*yu*) is homonymously used here for abundance 餘 (*yu*) and lotus 蓮 (*lien*) represents succession 連 (*lien*).

58
連年有餘
這兒「魚」用作「餘」,「蓮」用作「連」是同音的關係。

59-64
Folk Dances

59-64
民族舞蹈

91

65
Chang Kuo-lao
Of the Eight Immortals, three are historical figures and the remainder legendary. The have all for various reasons and in different ways achieved immortality. Chang Kuo-lao lived in the seventeenth century. He is depicted on his donkey, carrying a bamboo tube-drum which he beats with sticks. He is the patron of old men.

65
張果老
在八位仙人當中，三位是歷史人物，其餘的是傳奇人物。他們因各種理由和不同的途徑而升了仙。張果老活在十七世紀。他被描繪成一個騎在驢背上用棍子敲打着魚鼓的人。他是老人的庇護神。

66
Li Tieh-kuai
Another of the Eight Immortals, Li Tieh-kuai is represented as a lame beggar. He always carries with him an iron crutch and a gourd and rides an elephant. He is the patron of the sick.

66
李鐵拐
另一位八仙之一是李鐵拐，以跛脚乞丐的形象出現。他總是隨身帶着拐杖和葫蘆騎在象背上。他是不健全者的庇護神。

67
Cats and Butterfly
Both are suggestive of a long life. The cat 貓 (*mao*) is a pun on 耄 (*mao*), a person of eighty or ninety years. Butterfly 蝴蝶 (*hu tieh*) is used in the same way with 耋 (*tieh*), meaning a person of seventy or eighty years.

68
Gold Fish
Fish 魚 (*yu*) is similar in sound to abundance 餘 (*yu*) and here its scales have the colour of gold. It suggests an abundance of gold.

67
耄耋延年
貓蝶都含有長壽之意。「貓」是「耄」的雙關語，活到八十或九十歲的人稱爲「耄」。「蝴蝶」也以同樣的理由被用來表示「耋」的意思，即活到七十或八十歲的人。

68
金魚
「魚」跟「餘」同音，鱗呈金色。這兒牠含有金有餘的意思。

69
Mandarin Ducks
When depicted, as they often are, swimming in pairs they symbolise marital bliss.

70
Good Fortune and a Long Life
The bat 蝠 (*fu*) suggests good fortune 福 (*fu*) as does the Buddha's hand citrus 佛手 (*fo shou*). The peach symbolises longevity and the pomegranate, numerous offspring.

69
鴛鴦戲荷
鴛鴦被描繪成雙雙戲水，是象徵婚姻生活的至樂。

70
福壽長春
「蝠」和「佛手」的含義一樣，是「福」的意思。桃象徵長壽，石榴象徵百子千孫。

江蘇　Kiangsu
南京　Nanking
揚州　Yangchou

南京
Nanking

71
'May you live to a ripe old age'
The butterfly and cat again combine to bring this very acceptable and common birthday wish.

71
願君高壽
蝴蝶和貓可表示這個人們樂於接受的和一般的生日祝願。

72
Rooster
Symbol of reliability and courage

72
公雞
信賴與勇氣的象徵。

73
Mandarin Ducks
Symbols of fidelity and married bliss

73
鴛鴦
真誠與婚姻至樂的象徵。

74
'May you gain huge profits'
The carp 鯉 (*li*) represents profit 利 (*li*)

75
The Twin Immortals 'Harmony and Union'
Harmony 和 (*ho*) and union 合 (*ho*) are represented by a lotus 荷 (*ho*) and a box 盒 (*ho*), a complicated play on words and images which combine to mean concord. A persimmon is on the left, a *ju-i* on the right and a lotus-root are beneath the Immortals who are depicted as two youthful, laughing figures.

74
大吉大利
「鯉」象徵「利」。

75
和合雙仙
「和」跟「合」由「荷」跟「盒」來代表，是一個很複雜的雙關語，兩者合用意為「和諧」。柿子一個在左邊，如意則在右邊，放在雙仙下邊的是一條蓮藕。

76
'May you have noble sons'

77
Cowherd

76
貴子有餘

77
牧牛童

78
Carp
According to legend carp make an annual attempt to swim up the Yellow River towards the 'Dragon's Gate'. Those fish which succeed in battling against the rapids and arrive safely on the other side of the gate turn into dragons. The carp is thus the symbol of perseverance and passing the 'Dragon's Gate' carries with it the wish for passing examinations with distinction.

78
鯉躍龍門
根據傳說，鯉魚每年都競往黃河的龍門遊去。那些戰勝急流而安全抵達龍門彼岸的鯉魚就變爲龍。因此，鯉魚就是不屈不撓的象徵，同時，躍過「龍門」之說也含有以優越成績通過考試的意願。

79
Carp

80
Gold Fish
Gold fish 金魚 (*chin yu*) swimming in a pond 塘 (*t'ang*) suggests a hall filled with gold and jade 金玉滿堂 (*chin yu man t'ang*).

79
鯉魚

80
金玉滿堂
金魚游於塘中可作金玉滿堂之聯想。

81
Bird and Loquats

82
Hen and Chicks

81
小鳥枇杷

82
母雞和羣雛

83
Flowers and Birds

84
Swallows

83
花鳥知春

84
燕子

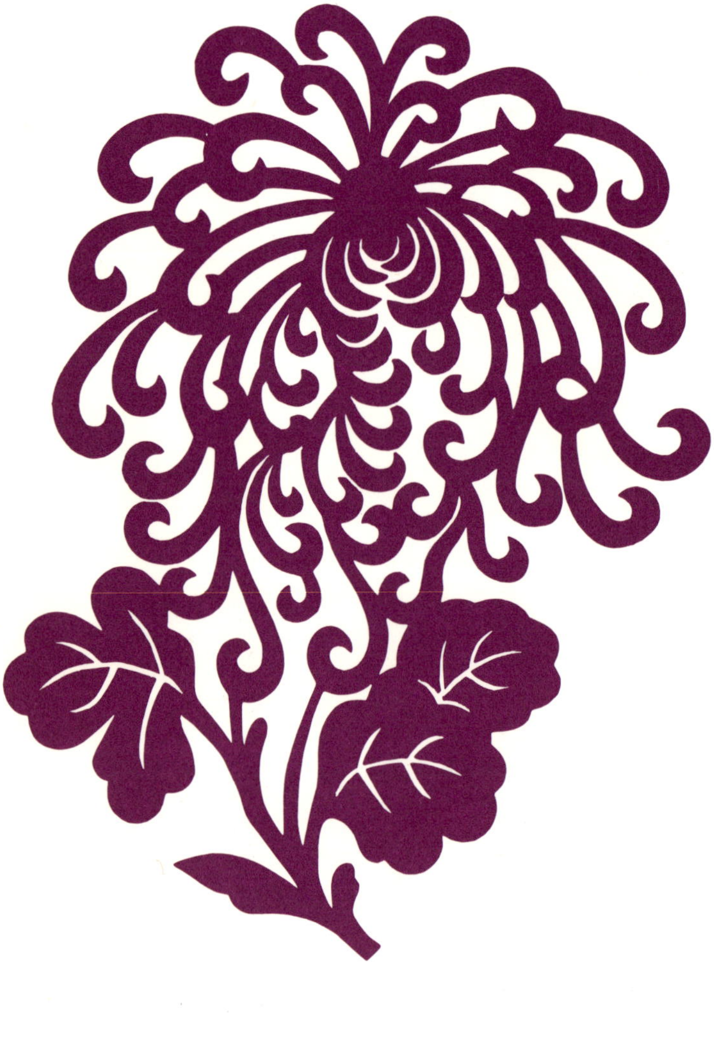

85-90
Chrysanthemum
Flower of autumn and symbol of
endurance

85-90
秋菊
秋菊是堅忍不拔的象徵。

揚州
Yangchou

91
Horse
The horse suggests stamina and speed. The papercut is based on the style of the painter Hsu Pei-hung (1895-1953).

91
馬到功成
馬可使人聯想到持久力與速度。這個剪紙是基於畫家徐悲鴻（1895—1953）的風格。

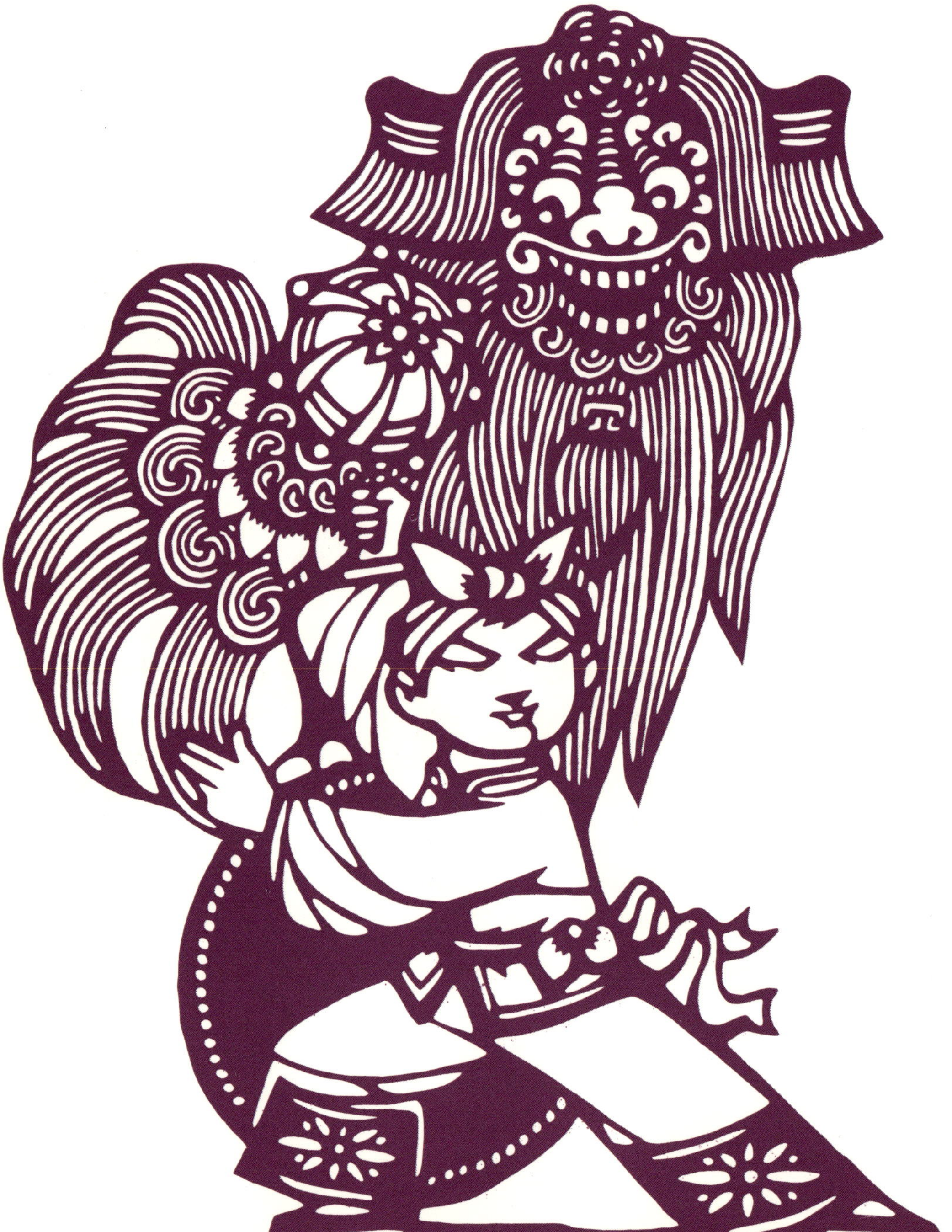

92-94
Lion Dance
In spite of its playful and mischievous nature, the lion symbolises valour and energy. Here it plays with an embroidered ball said originally to have been the Buddhist treasure.

92-94
獅子滾繡球
不管牠的滑稽和調皮的性情，獅子象徵英勇和活力。這兒是牠在玩弄一個象徵佛家之寶的繡球。

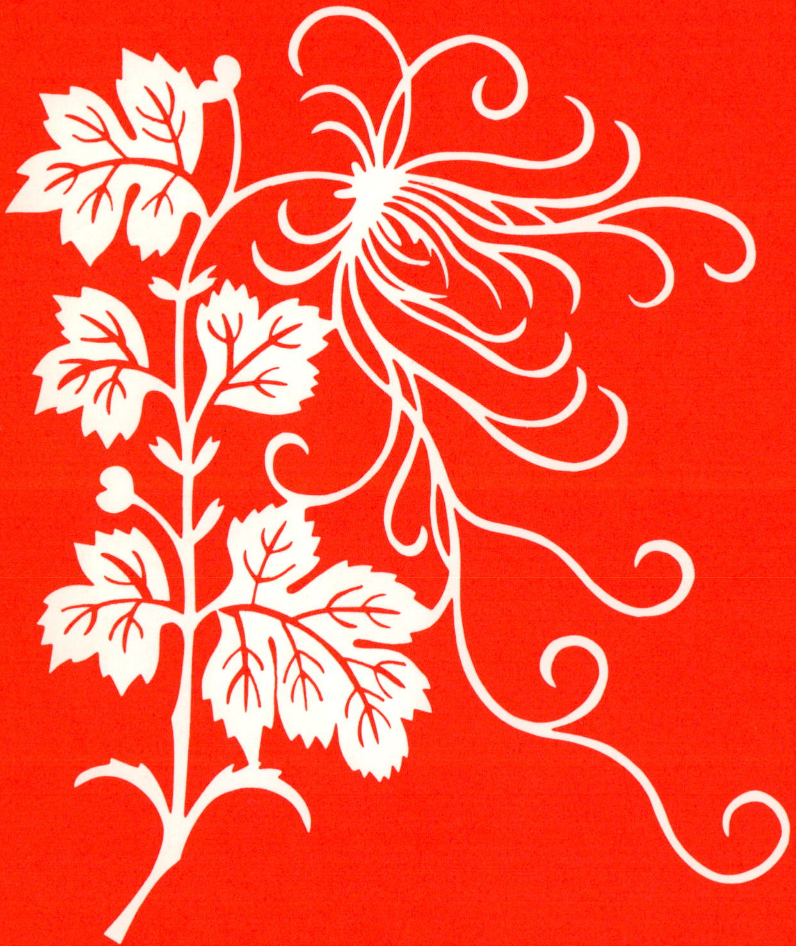
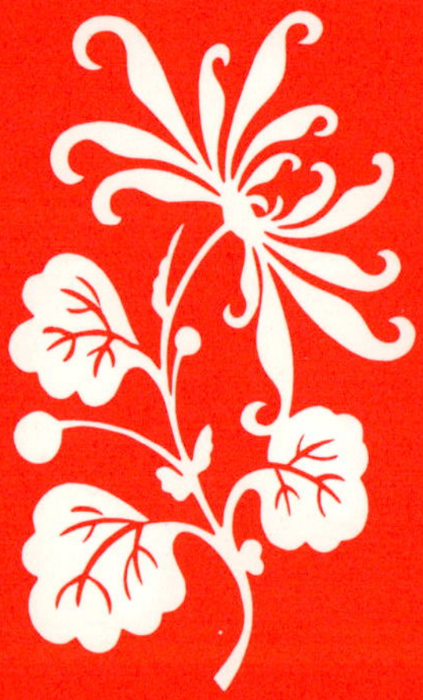
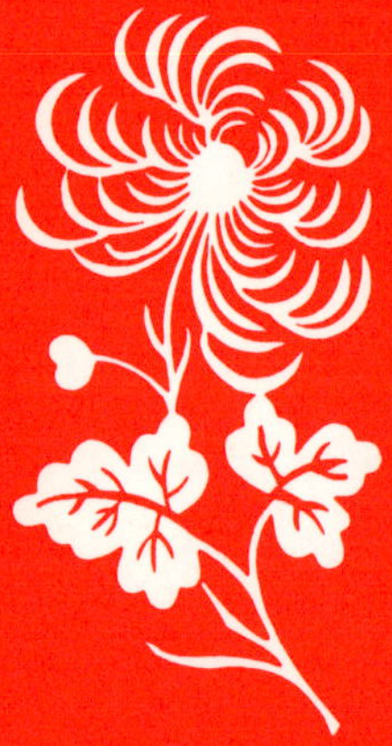

95-100
Chrysanthemum
Symbol of endurance and of enduring friendship

95-100
菊花
是堅忍不拔的象徵,也是恒久的友誼的象徵。

浙江　Chekiang
樂清　Loching
玉環　Yuhuan
其他地方　Other Places

樂清
Loching

101
Pine and Crane
The evergreen pine suggests constancy in friendship. Both the crane and the pine which have long life spans, symbolise a fabulous old age. This papercut is in the shape of a fan.

101
松鶴長春
常青的松使人聯想到友誼的永恆不變。長壽的松和鶴是象徵人可活到一個驚人的老年歲數。這個剪紙是扇形的。

102
Sewing

102
縫紉

103-105
Bumper Harvest

103-105
喜豐收

106
Phoenix and Peony
The mythical phoenix is a symbol of femininity. The peony represents riches and nobility.

107
Mandarin Ducks and Lotus
Symbol of harmony in marriage. The border is decorated with bamboo, pine, plum, magpies and a crane.

106
鳳凰牡丹
只存在於神話中的鳳凰是女子氣質的象徵。而牡丹則代表富貴。

107
鴛鴦戲荷
象徵婚姻生活的和諧。框邊有竹、松、梅、喜鵲和鶴。

108
Boy with Peony
The bats 蝠 (*fu*) used in the border are symbolic of good luck 福 (*fu*).

109
Carp
A pair of carp 鯉魚 (*li yu*) suggest double profit 利 (*li*) or abundance 餘 (*yu*). The border is decorated with squirrels and grapes, the tendrils of which symbolise continuity.

108
小童與牡丹
邊緣的「蝠」是「福」的象徵。

109
雙鯉
「雙鯉」使人聯想到「雙利」或「餘」。框邊有松鼠和葡萄，葡萄的卷鬚象徵持續不斷。

110
Welding

110
燒焊

111
Projectionist

111
電影播放員

125

112-114
Diving

112-114
跳水

126

115, 116
Gymnastics

115, 116
自由體操

玉環
Yuhuan

117
View of the West Lake

117
西湖景色

118
View of the West Lake

118
西湖景色

119
View of the West Lake

119
西湖景色

120
Altar of Prayer for Harvest,
Temple of Heaven, Peking

120
北京天壇祈年殿

121
Marble Boat, Summer Palace, Peking

121
北京頤和園石舫

122
Peach
One of the 'three blessings' the peach is symbolic of long life. According to legend Hsi Wang Mu, the Queen Mother of the West, is believed to guard the peaches of immortality which grow in her garden.

123
Radish
The red colour of the radish is symbolic of joy and festive occasions.

122
仙桃
被作爲三大祝福之一的仙桃是長壽的象徵。根據傳說，西王母是長在她園中的永生不滅的桃子的護衛者。

123
紅蘿蔔
紅蘿蔔的紅顏色是歡慶節日的象徵。

124
Carp
The carp 鯉 (*li*) suggests profit 利 (*li*).

125
Pig
The pig is a symbol of fertility.

124
鯉魚
「鯉」可聯想到「利」。

125
豬
豬是家肥屋潤的象徵。

其他地方
Other Places

126
Double Happiness
The two characters are those for double happiness. On each side are messengers of joy, magpies. Above are pomegranates, symbolising numerous offspring and below a pair of persimmons 柿子 (*shih tzu*) identified with good luck in business 事 (*shih*).

126

雙喜臨門
兩個喜字合並表示「雙喜」。在每一邊上都有喜鵲。上頭是石榴，象徵百子千孫。下面是兩個柿子，表示事事如意。

127
Stag
The stag is often grouped with another symbol of longevity, the pine. Its name 鹿 (*lu*) also suggests official income 祿 (*lu*).

127
鹿
鹿常常與另一個長壽象徵松放在一起。鹿的稱謂也可使人聯想到官俸，即祿。

128
Landscape
River scene with boats and a pagoda

128
風景
有船和塔的河流景色。

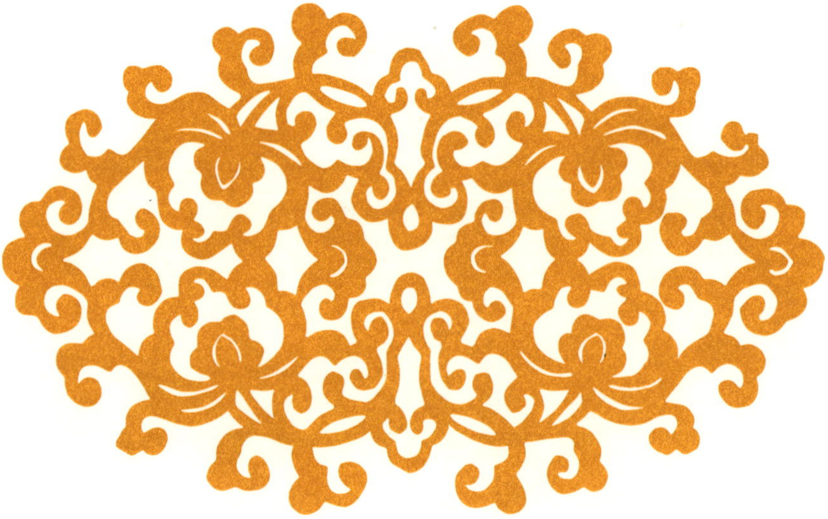

129-134
'Happy Flowers'

129-134
喜花

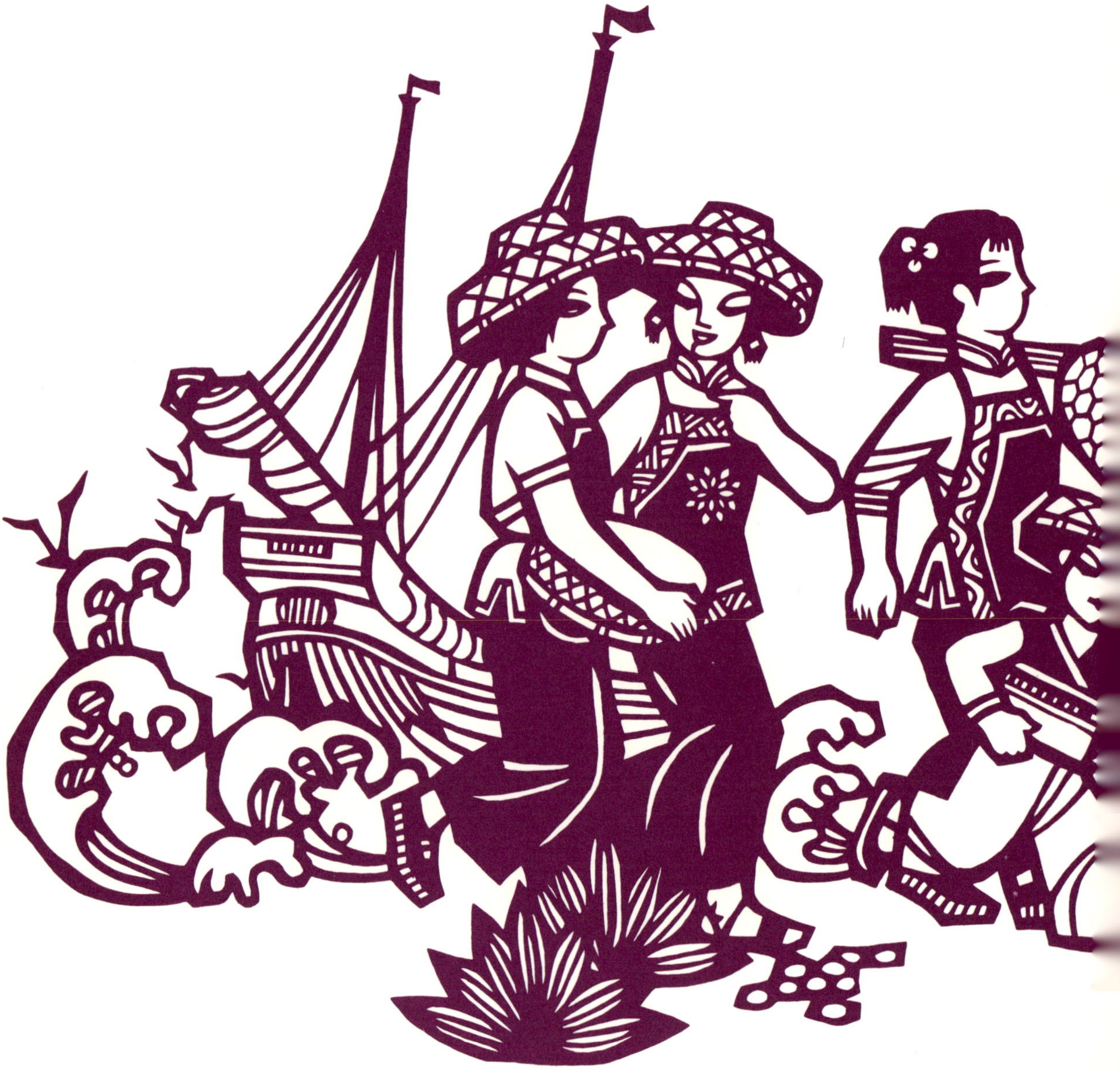

135
Fisherwomen

135
漁村婦女

136
Sampan Boat

136
舢舨

137
Bridge and Trees

137
橋與樹

138
'Happy Flowers'
Chrysanthemum and Lotus

138
喜花
菊與蓮

139
Botanists

139
植物學家

福建　Fukien
夏門　Amoy
泉州　Chuanchou

夏門
Amoy

**140
Sung Chiang,
Hero from** *The Water Margin*

**140
宋江**
「水滸」中的英雄。

141, 142
Liu T'ang and Li K'uei
Heros from *The Water Margin*

141, 142
赤髮鬼劉唐和黑旋風李逵
「水滸」中的英雄

143, 144
Madam Sun and Han T'ao
Heroine and hero from *The Water Margin*

143, 144
母夜叉孫二娘和百勝將韓滔
「水滸」中的英雄。

泉州
Chuanchou

145
Butterfly and Orchid
The butterfly, suggests long life while the orchid adds fragrance and refinements to the wish.

145
蝴蝶蘭花
蝴蝶可使人聯想到長壽,而蘭花則使人倍覺芬芳與雅緻。

146
Chrysanthemum
Resilient flower of autumn, symbol of endurance

147
Double Happiness

146
菊花
經久活色生香的秋菊是堅忍不拔的象徵。

147
雙喜臨門

148
Phoenix and Peony
The peony is the flower of spring and is symbolic of wealth. The phoenix is the symbol of femininity.

148
鳳凰牡丹
牡丹春天開花，是富有的象徵。
鳳凰是女子氣質的象徵。

廣東　Kwangtung
佛山　Foshan
潮州　Chaochou

佛山
Foshan

149
Stag and Peach Tree
Two symbols of longevity, one which lives to a great age and the other which holds the secret of immortality.

149
鹿與桃樹
兩者都是長壽的象徵，一個象徵是指活到高齡，另一個象徵是指把握住永生不滅的秘訣。

150
'Hundred Flowers Bloom'

150
百花齊放

151
Abundant Harvest

151
慶豐收

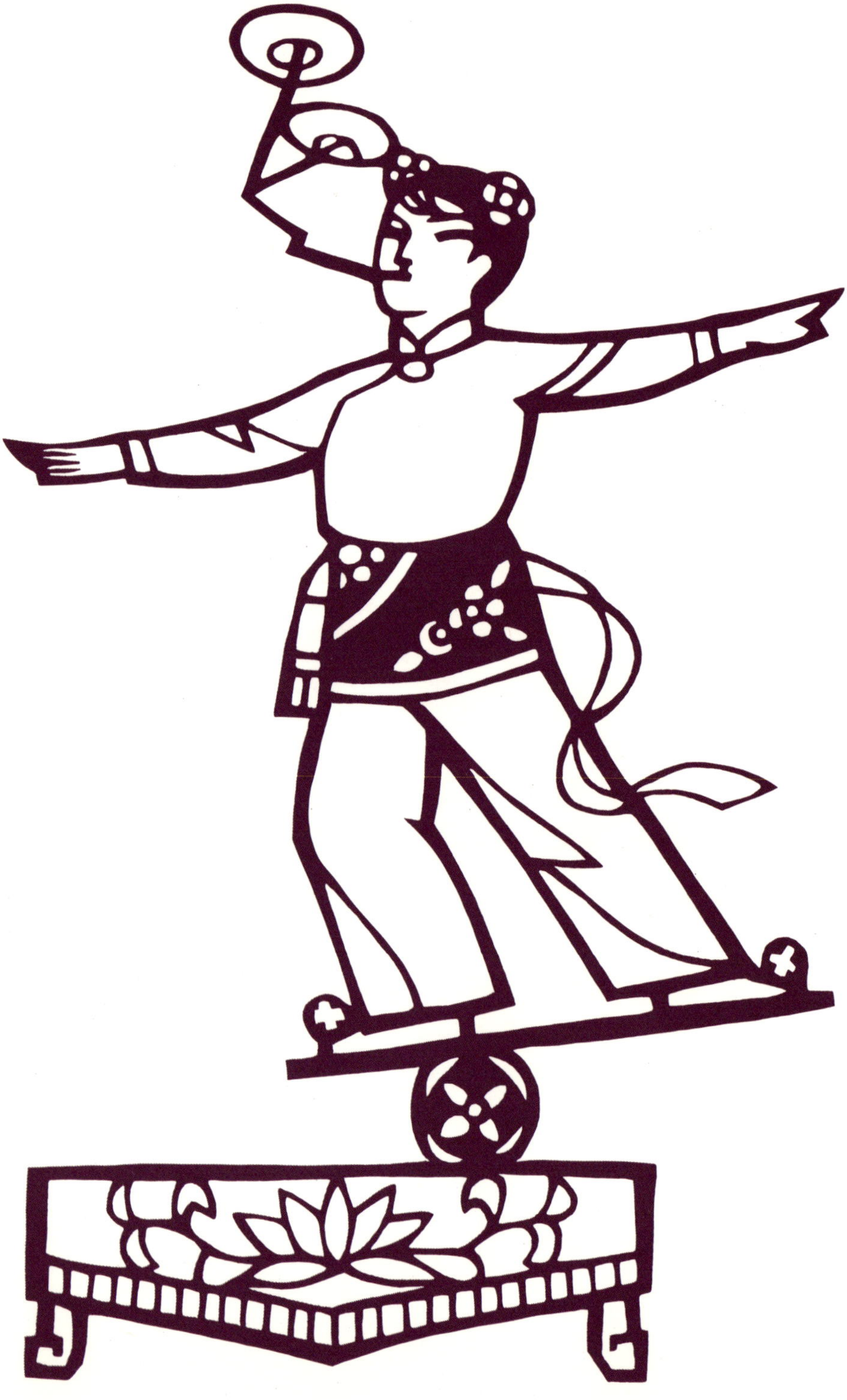

152-154
Acrobats

152-154
雜技

155-157
Lanterns

155-157
花燈

167

158
General Store

158
雑貨店

169

159
Doves
Symbol of faithfulness

160
Phoenix and Peony
The symbol of femininity with the flower of spring

161
Lotus
The fact that the buds, blossoms and seed pods can be seen at the same time has made the lotus an emblem of past, present and future.

162
Peony
The king of flowers is symbolic of riches and nobility.

163
Orchid
Symbol of love and beauty suggesting a life full of fragrance and refinement.

164
Chrysanthemum
The emblem of autumn

159
鴿子
忠誠可靠的象徵

160
鳳凰牡丹
象徵女子氣質的鳳凰與春之花牡丹。

161
蓮
蓓蕾、花朵和籽莢可在同一時間被人看見，所以蓮是能體現過去、現在和未來的象徵。

162
牡丹
這個萬花之王是富與貴的象徵。

163
蘭
愛情和美麗的象徵，可使人聯想到一個充滿芬芳和雅緻的生活。

164
菊
秋的象徵。

161

163

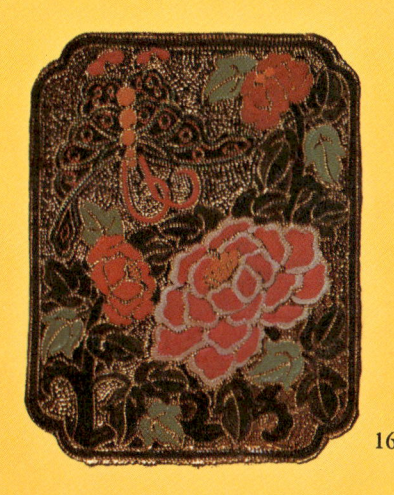

162

164

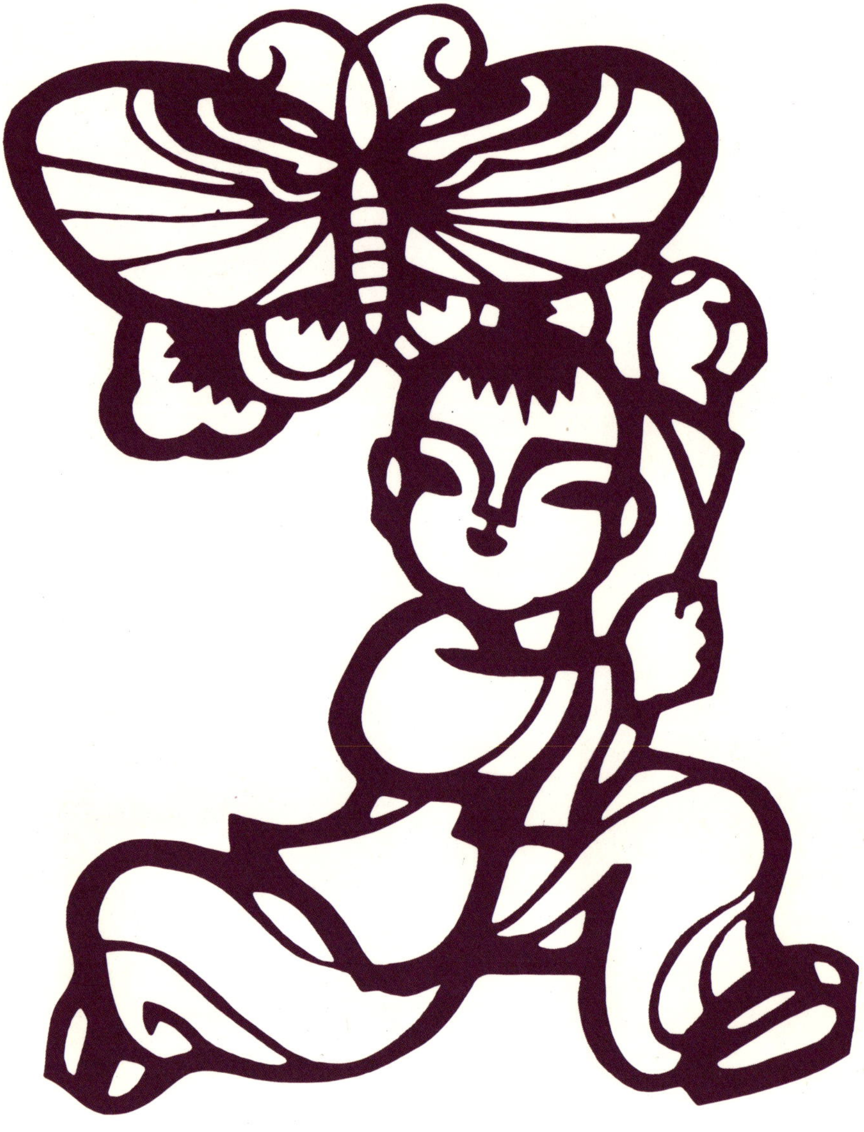

165-168
Kite Flying

165-168
放風箏

169-171
Ping-pong

172
Lotus and Dove

173
Spinning

174
Fish and Flowers

175
Peach

176
Good Harvest

169-171
乒乓球

172
蓮與鴿

173
紡織

174
魚兒花朵

175
桃子

176
豐收

170

174   171

172

173

174

175

176

潮州
Chaochou

**177
Two Lovers**
Liang visiting his beloved, a scene from *Liang Shan-pa and Chu Ying-tai*

177
梁祝相會
「梁山伯與祝英台」之一景。

177

178
Rooster
Its name 公雞 (*kung chi*) and the crow of the cock 鳴 (*ming*) suggest high honour 功名 (*kung ming*).

178
公雞
公雞之鳴可使人聯想到崇高的功名。

179
Phoenix and Peony
The symbols of femininity and wealth

179
鳳凰牡丹
女子氣質與富有的象徵。

180
Bamboo and Birds
The bamboo because of its strength, height, durability and evergreen qualities is an obvious symbol of longevity.

180
竹與鳥
因為具有堅韌、崇高、耐用和常青的品質，竹是長壽的明顯象徵。

181
Magpies and Plum Flowers
The bird of joy with the flower of spring

181
喜鵲梅花
鵲報喜，梅報春。

182
Flowers and Birds

182
花鳥知春

183
Rooster, Hen and Chicks
Here the name for rooster, hen and chicks 鷄 (*chi*) is used homonymously for auspicious 吉 (*chi*).

183
如意吉祥
公雞、母雞和小雞的名稱都有一個「雞」字，與「吉」字同音，表示吉祥。

184
Boy with Horse Lantern
Lanterns in all forms are used in lantern festivals. The horse lantern is in two parts, head and rear, each part being attached to the waist of a boy who walks in between. Each end is lit by a candle.

184
腰繫馬燈籠的小童
所有各色各樣的燈籠都是燈節派用場的。馬燈籠分爲頭尾兩截，分別繫在小童腰間的前後以便行走。前後兩端都各有一枝點着的蠟燭。

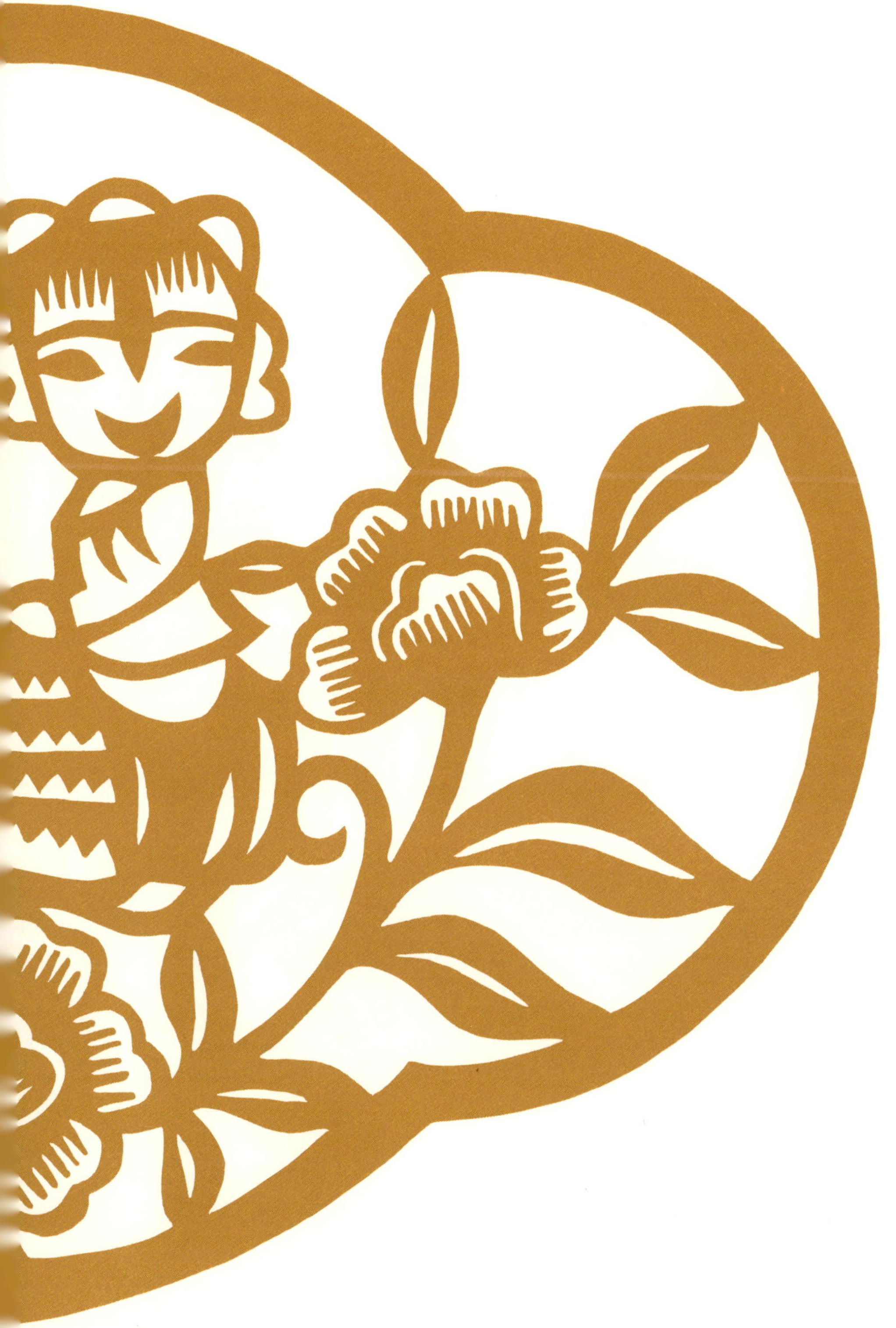

Acknowledgement 鳴謝

It is thanks to Ms. C.F. Bieber of Santa Fe, New Mexico that we came to know of the photographs of the craftsman making papercuts which appear here. These photographs were taken in the streets of Peking by Hedda Morrison in 1935 when she was working with Ms. Bieber. The photographs are reproduced with the kind permission of Hedda Morrison.

本書內有關一個剪紙藝人在工作的幾張圖片的收藏處，是全賴新墨西哥州聖提費市的比貝爾女士的賜知，我們謹向她致謝。這些圖片是一九三五年由海黛‧馬禮遜女士在北京街頭拍攝下來的，當時她和比貝爾女士在一起工作。這些圖片是在海黛‧馬禮遜的同意下複印的。

Index 索引

The number of the illustrations is printed in italics
插圖編號用斜體數字表示

動物 ANIMALS
- 蝠 Bat, 95 *70*, 123 *108*
- 水牛 Buffalo, 103 *77*
- 駱駝 Camel, 62 *31*, 74 *43*
- 貓 Cat, 94 *68*, 99 *71*
- 麒麟 *Chi-lin*, 41 *6*
- 狗 Dog, 57, *28*
- 驢 Donkey, 56 *27*, 65 *92*, 92 *65*
- 龍 Dragon, 37 *1*, 70 *37*
- 象 Elephant, 93 *66*
- 馬 Horse, 63 *32*, 111 *91*
- 獅 Lion, 57 *28*, 112, 113 *92-94*
- 猴 Monkey, 65 *34*, *35*
- 猪 Pig, 48 *19*, 135 *125*
- 松鼠 Squirrel, 123 *109*
- 鹿 Stag, 81 *51*, 138 *127*, 161 *149*
- 虎 Tiger, 71 *38*

雀鳥 BIRDS
- 鳥 Birds, 52 *21*, 106 *81*, 107 *83*, 180 *180*, 182 *182*
- 鷄 Chicken, 78 *47*, 106 *82*, 183 *183*
- 鶴 Crane, 119 *101*, 122 *107*
- 鴿子 Dove, 170 *159*, 175 *172*
- 喜鵲 Magpie, 54 *25*, 86 *54*, 122 *107*, 137 *126*, 181 *181*
- 鴛鴦 Mandarin Duck 95 *69*, 101 *73*, 122 *107*
- 雉鷄 Pheasant, 69 *36*, 72 *39*
- 鳳 Phoenix, 87 *56*, 122 *106*, 157 *148*, 170 *160*, 179 *179*
- 公鷄 Rooster, 64 *33*, 100 *72*, 178 *178*, 183 *183*
- 燕子 Swallow, 107 *84*

187

中國文字	**CHINESE CHARACTERS**
中國文字	Chinese Characters, 45 *15*, 47 *18*, 49 *20*, 134 *122*, 137 *126*, 162 *150*
雙喜	Double Happiness, 45 *15*, 137 *126*, 156 *147*

魚類	**FISH**
鯉	Carp, 102 *74*, 104 *78*, 105 *79*, 123 *109*, 135 *124*
魚	Fish, 85 *53*, 89 *58*, 175 *174*
金魚	Goldfish, 94 *68*, 105 *80*

喜花	**HAPPY FLOWERS**
喜花	Happy flowers, 140 *141* *129-134*, 146 *138*
百花齊放	Hundred Flowers Bloom, 162 *150*

昆蟲	**INSECT**
蝴蝶	Butterfly, 94 *68*, 99 *71*, 155 *145*

傳奇人物	**LEGENDARY CHARACTERS**
韓滔	Han T'ao, 153 *144*
李逵	Li K'uei, 152 *142*
劉唐	Liu T'ang, 152 *141*
孫二娘	Madam Sun, 153 *143*
宋江	Sung Chiang, 151 *140*

神話人物　　MYTHOLOGICAL CHARACTERS
　張果老　　Chang Kuo-lao,　92 *65*
　八仙　　　Eight Immortals,　92 *65*, 93 *66*
　財神　　　God of Wealth,　47 *17*, 49 *20*
　西王母　　Hsi Wang Mu,　134 *122*
　李鐵拐　　Li Tieh-kuai,　93 *66*
　孫悟空　　Monkey King　75 *44*
　神話人物　Mythological Characters,　60 *29*, 61 *30*, 74 *42*
　猪八戒　　Pig God,　75 *45*
　和合雙仙　Twin Immortals,　102 *75*

物件　　　　OBJECTS
　籃子　　　Basket,　39 *3*
　繡球　　　Brocade ball,　112, 113 *92-94*
　燭臺　　　Candlesticks,　45 *15*
　錢幣　　　Coins,　45 *15*, 47 *17*, 48 *19*, 49 *20*
　無盡結　　Endless knot,　45 *15*
　紅熔之珠　Flaming pearl,　37 *1*
　錠　　　　Ingot,　45 *15*, 46 *16*, 48 *19*
　如意　　　*Ju-i*,　45 *15*, 102 *75*
　風箏　　　Kites,　172, 173 *165-168*
　花燈　　　Lanterns,　65 *35*, 166, 167 *155-157*, 184, 185 *184*
　搖錢樹　　Moneytree,　49 *20*
　京劇臉譜　Opera masks,　42 *7-10*
　笙　　　　Organ,　41 *6*
　塔　　　　Pagoda,　129 *117*, 139 *128*
　吊錢　　　Pendant,　46 *16*, 47 *17-18*
　舢舨　　　Sampan boat,　144 *136*
　花瓶　　　Vase,　84 *52*

189

人物	PEOPLE
雜技員	Acrobats, 164, 165 *152-154*
植物學家	Botanist, 147 *139*
男童	Boy, 41 *6*, 88 *57*, 89 *58*, 123 *108*, 184, 185 *184*
牧牛童	Cowherd, 103 *77*
跳水健兒	Divers, 126 *112-114*
漁翁	Fisherman, 80 *50*
漁村婦女	Fisherwoman, 142, 143 *135*
民族舞蹈	Folk dances, 90, 91 *59-64*, 112, 113 *92-94*
少女	Girl, 56 *27*
自由體操	Gymnastics, 127 *115, 116*
放風箏	Kite-flying, 172, 173 *165-168*
乒乓	Ping Pong 174 *169-171*
電影播放員	Projectionist, 125 *111*
縫紉	Sewing, 120 *102*
紡織	Spinning, 79 *48*, 175 *173*
燒焊	Welding, 124 *110*

名勝古蹟	PLACES
北京石舫	Marble Boat, Peking, 133 *131*, 137 *126*, 181 *181*
頤和園	Summer Palace, 133 *121*
天壇祈年殿	Temple of Heaven, 132 *120*
西湖	West Lake, 129-131 *117-119*
黃河	Yellow River, 104 *78*

植物	PLANTS
竹	Bamboo, 122 *107*, 180 *180*
盆景	Bonsai, 53 *22-24*

佛手	Buddha's hand citron,	39 *3*, 95 *70*
豐收	Bumper harvest,	121 *103-105*, 163 *151*
菊	Chrysanthemum,	40 *4*, 47 *17*, *18*, 108, 109 *85-90*, 114, 115 *95-100*, 146, *138*, 156 *146*,
花	Flowers,	39 *3*, 52 *21*, 84 *52*, 107 *83*, 175 *174*, 182 *182*
水果	Fruit,	39 *3*, 106 *81*
葫蘆	Gourd,	38 *2*, 93 *66*
葡萄	Grape,	123 *109*
豐收	Harvest,	121 *103-105*, 163 *151*, 175 *176*
蓮	Lotus,	41 *6*, 45 *15*, 85 *53*, 88 *57*, 89 *58*, 102 *75*, 122 *107*, 146 *138*, 171 *161*, 175 *172*
桑	Mulberry tree,	77 *46*
蘭	Orchid,	55 *26*, 155 *145*, 171 *163*
桃	Peach,	39 *3*, 95 *70*, 134 *122*, 175 *175*
桃樹	Peach tree,	161 *149*
牡丹	Peony,	40 *5*, 87 *56*, 122 *106*, 123 *108*, 157 *148*, 170 *160*, 171 *162*, 179 *179*
柿子	Persimmon,	102 *75*, 137 *126*
松	Pine,	119 *101*, 122 *107*, 138 *127*
梅	Plum blossom,	86 *54*, 122 *107*, 181 *181*
石榴	Pomegranate,	39 *3*, 86 *55*, 95 *70*, 137 *126*
紅蘿蔔	Radish,	134 *123*
樹	Trees,	145 *137*

戲劇人物 THEATRICAL CHARACTERS

祝英台	Chu Ying-tai,	177 *177*
梁山伯	Liang Shan-pa,	177 *177*
穆桂英	Mu Kwei-ying,	72 *39*
京劇臉譜	Opera masks,	42 *7-10*
戲劇人物	Theatrical Characters,	43 *11-14*, 73 *40*, *41*